REACHING OLYMPUS
TEACHING MYTHOLOGY THROUGH READER'S THEATER SCRIPT-STORIES

HERO TALES
FROM WORLD MYTHOLOGY

WRITTEN AND ILLUSTRATED BY
ZACHARY HAMBY

EDITED BY
RACHEL HAMBY

DEDICATION

In memory of Jacob Key

"The world is indeed full of peril, and in it there are many dark places.
But still there is much that is fair."
-J.R.R. Tolkien-

"Where we had thought to be alone, we shall be with all the world."
-Joseph Campbell-

ISBN-10: 0-9827049-8-4
ISBN-13: 978-0-9827049-8-1

Hero Tales from World Mythology: Teaching World Mythology through
Reader's Theater Script-Stories
Written and Illustrated by Zachary Hamby
Edited by Rachel Hamby
Published by Hamby Publishing in the United States of America

Copyright © 2023 Hamby Publishing

All rights reserved. Portions of this book may be photocopied for classroom use only. No portion of this book may be reproduced in any form or by any electronic or mechanical means, including information storage and retrieval systems, without permission in writing from the publisher, except by a reviewer, who may quote brief passages in review. Special permissions are required for commercial or public performances of these scripts. Contact the author for more information about the fees associated with these types of performances.

TABLE OF CONTENTS

INTRODUCTORY MATERIALS

Introduction to the Series	7
Using This Book in the Classroom	11
The Hero with Many Faces	13

SCRIPT-STORIES: HERO TALES FROM WORLD MYTHOLOGY

Lugalbanda the Littlest Prince	15
Li Chi and the Serpent	31
Momotaro the Peach Boy	45
Anansi and the Sky God's Stories	61
Vasilisa the Brave	73
The Deeds of Finn Mac Cool	85
Grandfather Chenoo	99
The Hero Twins in the Land of the Dead	113
The Magic Lake	127
Maui the Mighty	141

SUPPLEMENTAL MATERIALS

Design-a-Quest	155

APPENDICES

About the Author   157

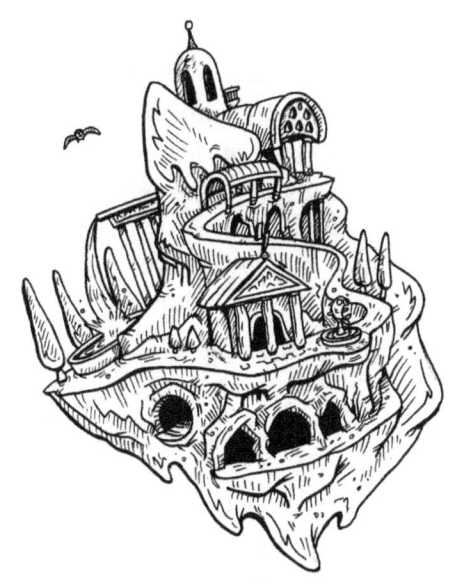

REACHING OLYMPUS:
AN INTRODUCTION TO THE SERIES

The faces of the souls of the underworld could not have been more death-like. It was years ago, but I remember it well. In a matter of weeks, I had gone from inexperienced student to full-time teacher. Smack dab in the midst of my student teaching experience, I was asked to take over as the classroom teacher. Even more startling: Four long years of college had not prepared me for the subject matter I would be required to teach—a class called World Short Stories and (gulp) Mythology. I remembered a few short stories from my survey literature courses, but with mythology, I was drawing a blank. In my cobwebbed memory there stood a woman with snake-hair and a psychedelic image of a wingéd horse—but that was it. Not to worry though. I had two whole weeks to prepare. After that I needed to fill a whole semester with mythological learning.

As any competent educator would, I turned to my textbook for aid. At first things looked promising. The book had a classy cover—black with the before-mentioned wingéd horse on it. Bold gold letters tastefully titled it *Mythology*. Edith Hamilton—in the same lettering—was apparently the author. Yes, my judgment of the cover was encouraging, but what I found inside was anything but.

When I opened the text to read, I quickly realized I was doomed. Edith Hamilton had written her book in code. It was the same indecipherable language used by those who write literary criticism or owner manuals for electronic devices. Every sentence was a labyrinth, curving back in on itself, confusing the reader with many a subordinate clause and cutting him off completely from context with an outdated aphorism. If she wasn't randomly quoting Milton or Shakespeare, she was spending a paragraph differentiating between the poetic styles of Pindar and Ovid. It was as if Edith Hamilton was annoyed at having been born in the twentieth century and was using her writing style as some kind of literary time travel. Originally published in 1942, *Mythology* reflects the writing style of the day—a style that has grown increasingly more difficult for modern readers to comprehend. I knew if I could barely understand Hamilton's language, my students were going to be even more lost than I was.

Designed for average learners, Mythology was a junior-senior elective—the kind of class that was supposed to be entertaining and somewhat interesting. With Edith Hamilton tied around my neck, I was going down—and going down fast. It was at this point that the stupidly optimistic part of my brain cut in. "Maybe it won't be so bad," it said. "Don't underestimate your students." My ambitions renewed thanks to this still, small voice, and I laid Hamilton to the side, somehow sure that everything would turn out all right in the end. This was still more proof that I knew nothing about mythology.

Before I continue to tell how my tragic flaw of youthful optimism led to my ultimate downfall, I should take a minute to say a kind word about Edith Hamilton. In a time when interest in the classical writings of Greece and Rome was waning, Edith Hamilton revitalized this interest by writing several works that attempted to capture the creativity and majesty of Greco-Roman civilization. Hamilton's *Mythology* was one of the first books to take a comprehensive look at the Greco-Roman myths. The popularity of mythology today owes a great deal of debt to this book and its author. Fifty years after its publication, it is still the most commonly used mythology textbook in high school classrooms. Ironically, *Mythology* is no longer on an average high-schooler's reading level. As I mentioned earlier, Hamilton's writing style, with its ponderous vocabulary and sphinx-worthy inscrutability, further alienates any but the most intrepid of readers.

My first semester of teaching Mythology was a disaster. If I hadn't been so idealistic and gung-ho, I probably would have given up. Instead the new teacher within me stood up and said, "No! I'm going to do this, and we're going to make it fun! After all, Mythology is filled with all kinds of teenage interests: family murder, bestiality, incest, etc. It'll be just like watching television for them."

Utilizing every creative project idea under the sun, I threw myself into making the class work. We drew pictures, read aloud, watched related videos, wrote alternate endings to the stories—yet every time I kept coming up against the same brick wall: the text. It did not matter how enjoyable the activities were. Whenever we turned to the actual stories and cracked open that dreaded book, the life was sucked out of my students, and I was staring at their underworld faces once again.

My last resort was boiling the stories down to outlines and writing these out on the whiteboard. Even that was better than actually reading them. At least the students would get the basic facts of the story. One student, possibly sensing I was seconds away from the breaking point, made the comment, "I didn't know this class would be a bunch of notes. I thought it would be fun."

Then I gave up. When I look back on that semester, I realize that I failed a whole batch of students. They came and went thinking that studying mythology was a brainless exercise in rote memorization. Perhaps the failure of that first experience would not have been so stark if a success hadn't come along the next year.

The second time through the class, I was determined not to repeat the mistakes of the past. There must be some way of avoiding the text—somehow relating the stories without actually reading them. But then I thought, "Isn't this supposed to be an English class? If we don't actually read, can it be called English? What has this outdated text driven me to?"

When I looked into the stories, I could see excellent tales trapped behind stuffy prose. How could I get the students to see what I saw? How could I set those good stories free?

On a whim I decided to try my hand at rewriting one of the myths. I had dabbled in creative writing in college, so surely I could spin one of these tales better than Edith Hamilton had. The idea of dividing the story into parts struck me as a good one. Maybe that would foster more student involvement. A few hours later, I had created my first Reader's Theater script-story. (At the time I had no idea that there was an actual term for this type of thing or that there was sound educational research behind reading aloud.) Part of me was excited. The other part was skeptical. "These kids are high-schoolers," I said to myself. "They'll never go for this." I looked at some of the elements I had included in my script: overly-dramatic dialogue, sound effects, cheesy jokes. What was I thinking? Since I had already spent the time and energy, I decided to give it a shot.

There are those grand moments in education when something clicks, and those moments are the reason that teachers teach. My script clicked. It clicked quite well, in fact. The students loved reading aloud. They were thrilled beyond belief not to be reading silently or taking notes or even watching a video. They performed better than I ever dreamed possible. They did funny voices. They laughed at the cheesy jokes. They inhabited the characters. They even did the sound effects.

As I looked around the room, I noticed something that was a rarity: My students were having fun. Not only that, but they were getting all the information that Edith Hamilton could have offered them. When the script was done, I encountered a barrage of questions: "Why did Zeus act like that to Hera? What is an heir? Why did Aphrodite choose to marry Hephaestus? Did the Greeks have *any* respect for marriage?" Did my ears deceive me? Intelligent questions—questions about character motivation, vocabulary, and even historical context? I couldn't believe it.

I was also struck by another startling fact: The students were asking about these characters as if they were real people. They were able to treat the characters as real people because real people had inhabited their roles. Zeus was not some dusty god from 3,000 years ago. He was Joe in the second row doing a funny voice. Something had come from the abstract world of mythology and become real. And as for the quiz scores, my students might not remember the difference between Perseus and Theseus, but they definitely remembered the difference between Josh and Eric, the two students who played those roles. On top of all this, the class had changed from a group of isolated learners to a team that experiences, laughs, and learns together.

After the success of that first script, I realized I had created some kind of teaching drug. It was an incredible experience, one that I wanted to recreate over and over again. I wouldn't and couldn't go back to the old world of bland reading. So I didn't.

The great moments of Greek mythology flew from my keyboard, and I created script after script. Despite my overweening enthusiasm, I knew that too much of a good thing could definitely be bad, so I chose stories that would spread out the read-aloud experience. We would still use Edith Hamilton in moderation. After all, a few vegetables make you enjoy the sweet stuff all the more.

Over the course of that semester, I discovered a new enthusiasm in the students and myself. They enjoyed learning, and I enjoyed teaching. I had students arguing over who would read which parts—an unbelievable sight for juniors and seniors. Laughter was a constant in the classroom. As the Greeks would say, it was a golden age of learning.

Now I have the chance to share this technique with other teachers. With these script-stories, I hope my experiences will be recreated in other classrooms. Mythology should not be an old dead thing of the past, but a living, breathing, exciting experience.

USING THIS BOOK IN THE CLASSROOM

Script-stories (also known as Reader's Theater) are a highly motivational learning strategy that blends oral reading, literature, and drama. Unlike traditional theater, script-stories do not require costumes, make-up, props, stage sets, or memorization. Only the script and a healthy imagination are needed. As students read the script aloud, they interpret the emotions, beliefs, attitudes, and motives of the characters. A narrator conveys the story's setting and action and provides the commentary necessary for the transitions between scenes.

While Reader's Theater has been enormously successful with lower grade-levels, it is a great fit for older learners as well. Students of any age enjoy and appreciate the chance to *experience* a story rather than having it read to them. For years now script-stories have been the tool that I use to teach mythology to high-schoolers. I wouldn't have it any other way. Below are the answers to some of the most frequently asked questions concerning the use of script-stories in the classroom.

How do you stage these stories in the classroom? Hand out photocopies of the particular script for that day. (Note: It is perfectly legal for you to photocopy pages from this book. That is what it was designed for!) Certain copies of the scripts should be highlighted for particular characters, so that whichever students you pick to read parts will have their lines readily available. (This is not necessary, but it does make things run more smoothly.) Some teachers who use script-stories require their students to stand when reading their lines or even incorporate physical acting. As for the sound effects in the scripts (*fanfare*), noisemakers can be distributed to the students and used when prompted. Otherwise, students can make the noises with their own voices.

How do you structure a class around script-stories? How often do you use them? Too much of a good thing can be bad. In my own classroom I do employ the script-stories frequently—in some units we read a story every day of the week—but I do supplement with other notes, texts, activities, and self-created worksheets. Some of these activities are included in the back of the book. For other examples of these activities, check out my website: Creative English Teacher.

How do you assess script-stories? A quick reading quiz after the completion of a script is an easy way to assess comprehension. In my own classroom I ask five questions that hit the high-points of the story. I never make the questions overly specific (for example, asking a student to remember a character's name like Agamemnon or Polydectes). Each script in this book comes with five recall questions for this purpose. Another form of assessment is by fostering as much classroom discussion as possible. How well students discuss will tell you how well they have comprehended the story. The discussion questions included in this book have seen success in my own classroom.

I hope you find this book to be a great resource. It was designed with the intent of helping a much wider audience experience the timeless tales of world mythology in a new manner. Below I have listed some further notes concerning the script-stories. Thanks for purchasing this book. Please feel free to contact me if you have any questions.

Sincerely,

Zachary Hamby
zachary@creativeenglishteacher.com
www.creativeenglishteacher.com

FURTHER NOTES FOR TEACHERS

UNIT PLAN: Teaching one of these scripts a day and including some of the suggested activities (see individual teacher pages) should yield at least an 11-day unit.

INTENDED AUDIENCE: 6-12th grade

LENGTH: Script-stories range between 25-45 minutes in length

SCRIPT-STORY PROCESS

- Every student will need a copy of the script-story.
- Reading parts may be highlighted for greater reading ease.
- As the teacher, you are the casting director. Assign the parts as you deem best.
- Give your largest parts to your strongest readers but still try to draw out the reluctant participant.
- As the teacher, you should take the part of the narrator. Actively participating only makes it more fun for you and the students.
- Cut loose and have fun. Script-stories allow students to see their teacher in a whole new light.

POSSIBLE MODIFICATIONS

- Costumes, props, and even sets can be added to any script-story to make it more engaging.
- Requiring the students to stand while reading their parts creates a stronger dynamic between speaking roles.
- Encouraging students to write their own script-stories gets them thinking about the elements of storytelling and the use of dialogue.
- Assigning one student to be responsible for all the sound effects in a script-story can involve someone who is not a strong reader in the performance. Including certain tools that actually make the indicated sound effects (noise-makers, whistles, coconuts, etc.) is another excellent way to add interest.

THE HERO WITH MANY FACES

It all started with Anansi. I grew up in a house full of books—wall-to-wall stories–and among these was one of my favorites, a brightly illustrated storybook of "Anansi and the Sky God's Stories." The story's central figure, Anansi, a trickster who is both spider and man, risks his life to climb into the heavens and meet face-to-face with the Sky God, a towering, intimidating deity. The story intrigued me not just because Anansi faces danger or travels into an unknown realm; many heroes had done the same. It was the object his quest. Anansi is not seeking treasure or fame. He is seeking stories. In the Sky God's palace is an unlimited supply of stories–piles and piles of them–but they are his and his alone. Anansi's bold request of the Sky God is that he share his stories with the humans of earth, who have none and as a result, live bland, pointless lives. The Sky God agrees, provided Anansi takes on a series of deadly tasks. Anansi uses his wits to complete these tasks and wins stories for mankind.

This story impacted me in multiple ways. First, it was my earliest experience with world mythology. Secondly, Anansi's world, a world without stories, seemed so strange, sad, and empty. Humans had nothing to give them joy—nothing to show them a way out when it seemed that there was none. Thirdly, Anansi's quest was worthy. Stories are a treasure. They can mean the difference between light and darkness, hope and despair. He was a hero for risking so much for humanity.

Since those early days, I have read hundreds of stories from many different cultures and discovered that the West African myth of Anansi is just a single thread in a vibrant tapestry of myths spanning the entire world. I have also learned that although these stories originate in cultures far removed from each other, both in location and worldview, they contain many common themes and patterns. After all, myths are reflections of the people who told them, and since the beginning of time, all peoples of the earth have experienced the same hopes, dreams, and fears. Ultimately, myths are proof that deep down, we human beings are more alike than we might think.

Foremost among these common elements is the archetype of the Hero, a brave character who selflessly undertakes a quest for the greater good of his or her people. No single culture can claim to have invented this character type because it is omnipresent. Each culture's heroes may have differing external features—or "faces" if you will—but the same heart beats within. A hero like Anansi is one of thousands.

Journeys play an important part in hero stories. Some heroes literally venture many miles along a dangerous road while others go on a journey of the soul—not physically travelling far but digging deeper into who they are and what they believe. Like heroes themselves, these journeys have cross-cultural commonalities, which myth researcher Joseph Campbell famously revealed in his book *The Hero with a Thousand Faces.* Campbell dubbed this worldwide storytelling pattern the monomyth or Hero's Journey, and it continues today in modern fiction, film, and video games. (To keep this storytelling tradition alive, the "Design-a-Quest" activity at the end of this book asks students create their own story based on the Hero's Journey.) A book on world mythology must provide a panorama of cultures. Therefore, the heroes found within have a variety of faces, their stories representing cultures from each inhabited continent.

- Lugalbanda the Littlest Prince (Mesopotamia)
- Li Chi and the Serpent (China)
- Momotaro the Peach Boy (Japan)
- Anansi and the Sky God's Stories (West Africa)
- Vasilisa the Brave (Russia)
- The Deeds of Finn Mac Cool (Ireland)
- Grandfather Chenoo (American Indian)
- The Hero Twins in the Land of the Dead (Mesoamerica)
- The Magic Lake (Ecuador)
- Maui the Mighty (Polynesia)

The final face to place upon the hero is our own. As we read hero stories, we adventure alongside them, learning from their successes and failures. Heroes challenge us. They change us. They spur us to do the difficult deeds that need to be done. Ultimately, heroes and their stories make us better people.

LUGALBANDA: THE LITTLEST PRINCE
TEACHER GUIDE

BACKGROUND

All stories from myth and legend are ancient. But some are more ancient than others, and this story earns the distinction of being the oldest. How so? When scholars make such a determination, they judge by the oldest written versions of the story. Like *The Epic of Gilgamesh*, another Mesopotamian myth, the story of Lugalbanda was written in cuneiform on stone tablets and only unearthed during the last century. Based on this evidence, the story of Lugalbanda dates back to 2,100 B.C. (beating out *Gilgamesh* by 100-300 years) to claim the title of the world's oldest hero story. Fittingly, Lugalbanda was the father of Gilgamesh.

The full story of Lugalbanda, whose name literally means "little prince," comes from two separate story fragments. One tells about Lugalbanda's journey toward Aratta, his sickness in the cave, and his deliverance from death by the gods. The second story deals with the episode of Lugalbanda and the Anzu bird.

Lugalbanda's story may be the oldest, but its plot is surprisingly fresh. Instead of destroying a monster, the little prince shows mercy, and instead of desiring war, he brings about peace. Young readers can still learn much from the oldest of stories.

SUMMARY

Lugalbanda is the youngest of the eight sons of King Enmerkar. The king spends all his time trying to please Inanna, the goddess of love and war, who is the secret of his success. When Inanna commands Enmerkar to attack the city of Aratta and steal its riches, the king mobilizes his army. Lugalbanda is excited because he is finally old enough to accompany the troops. However, as they enter the Zabu Mountains, which are home to many dangerous monsters, Lugalbanda begins to feel ill. His much-older brothers place him a cave and tend to him, but it seems he will soon die. Since the army must move on, they leave Lugalbanda with provisions in case he miraculously recovers.

When Lugalbanda awakens, he calls out to Shamash, the god of the sun, Inanna, the goddess of love, and Nana, the goddes of the moon, to save him. He recovers and continues on through the mountains. Soon he meets an Urmahlullu, a creature with the top half of a man and the bottom half of a lion. The Urmahlullu tells Lugalbanda that all the monsters of the mountains are afraid of Anzu, a half-lion, half-bird creature that is the king of the monsters. Soon after this Lugalbanda sees an enormous tree that is home to Anzu, and near it he discovers one of Anzu's chicks, who has fallen from the nest. Lugalbanda takes pity on the creature and carries it back to its high nest.

Anzu returns to the nest and, finding his chick safely returned, gives Lugalbanda the gift of incredible speed as a reward. Lugalbanda races over the mountains to where his father and brothers have beseiged the city of Aratta. When they tell him the war is not going well because Inanna has removed her support, Lugalbanda volunteers to run back to Uruk and speak to her. He does so and convinces the goddess to make peace with Aratta instead of destroying it. She tells Lugalbanda of a magic fish the king's soldiers should eat to give them strength to conquer Aratta. Lugalbanda bears this news back to his father, who catches the fish, conquers the city, and establishes peace between their cities. Lugalbanda is celebrated as a hero.

ESSENTIAL QUESTIONS

- Why should we have mercy on others?
- Does being the littlest mean you are the weakest?

NAME PRONUNCIATIONS

Anzu	AHN-ZU
Aratta	UH-RAH-TUH
Enmerkar	EN-MER-KAHR
Inanna	IH-NAH-NAH
Lugalbanda	LOO-GAHL-BAND-UH
Nana	NAH-NAH
Shamash	SHUH-MASH
Urmahlullu	ER-MUH-LOO-LOO
Uruk	OO-RUK
Zabu	ZAH-BOO

ANTICIPATORY QUESTIONS

- What are some of the most difficult parts of being young?
- Do younger siblings have it harder than older ones?

CREATURE FEATURE

Anzu Depicted as a giant bird with the head of a lion, Anzu was said to breathe fire and cause storms by simply flapping his wings. The gods gave him the job of protecting the Tablet of Destinies, which conferred supreme power upon its owner. But instead the wily creature stole it for himself. The archer-god Ninurta battled Anzu to recover the Tablet. At the end of this battle, some stories claim Anzu died, but in others the creature appears in the Zabu Mountains—possibly exiled for his crimes.

TEACHABLE TERMS

- **Theme: Mercy** Just as Lugalbanda has compassion on the baby Anzu bird, he also convinces Inanna to have mercy on the city of Aratta.
- **Culture: Lapis Lazuli** On pg. 18 Inanna covets the city of Aratta's supply of lapis lazuli, a stone noted for its deep blue color. Many ancient rulers desired it and established trade with other cities to obtain it.
- **Backstory** On pg. 20 one of Lugalbanda's brothers tells the backstory of Anzu.
- **Simile** On pg. 22 the narrator says Lugalbanda picked his way among the rocky peaks "like a wild horse."
- **Character Development** Although the Urmahlullu says, "monsters don't learn lessons" on pg. 25, Anzu's comments on pgs. 25-26 seem to indicate he has learned from his mistakes.

RECALL QUESTIONS

1. Why does King Enmerkar want to conquer the city of Aratta?
2. Why do Lugalbanda's brothers leave him behind as they journey to Aratta?
3. What does Lugalbanda do when he finds an Anzu chick in the mountains?
4. How does Lugalbanda gain incredible speed?
5. Inanna tells Lugalbanda his father's troops will be victorious if they do what?

LUGALBANDA THE LITTLEST PRINCE

CAST

LUGALBANDA	*Young Prince*
BROTHER ONE	*Lugalbanda's Brother*
BROTHER TWO	*Lugalbanda's Brother*
BROTHER THREE	*Lugalbanda's Brother*
BROTHER FOUR	*Lugalbanda's Brother*
BROTHER FIVE	*Lugalbanda's Brother*
BROTHER SIX	*Lugalbanda's Brother*
BROTHER SEVEN	*Lugalbanda's Brother*
ENMERKAR	*King of Uruk*
INANNA	*Fickle Goddess*
ANZU	*Giant, Winged Creature*
CHICK	*Baby Creature*
URMAHLULLU	*Strange Creature*

NARRATOR: Uruk was the mightiest city for miles around, and King Enmerkar was its powerful ruler. Everyone knew that the goddess Inanna favored him, and this was the secret of his success. Years before, she had appeared to the king in a vision.

INANNA: King Enmerkar, I am Inanna, the goddess of love and war.

ENMERKAR: Oh, yes! I recognize you from your statues.

INANNA: Drain the marsh between the Tigris and Euphrates Rivers, and there build a city worthy of me! I, Inanna, the Evening Star, have spoken!

ENMERKAR: Yes, noble goddess! It shall be as you say!

NARRATOR: Enmerkar's city had paved streets and beautiful buildings and the highest walls. The king built it so well that the goddess even descended to live there herself—atop the city's mighty temple.

Yet the king struggled to keep Inanna satisfied. As the goddess of love and war, it seemed she was always filled with either love or anger—never peace. The king was always searching for ways to make Uruk bigger and better, so Inanna's attentions did not stray elsewhere.

Meanwhile, Enmerkar had eight sons. The seven oldest were powerful warriors, who helped lead their father's army.

And then there was the eighth son, Lugalbanda, who was much younger—so young he did not fit in with his brothers.

BROTHER ONE: We're off to battle again, Lugalbanda. Don't worry though. Someday you will be old enough to fight like us.

LUGALBANDA: I'm old enough now. I want to help!

BROTHER TWO: Don't be silly, Lugalbanda. You're too young, but you'll grow up soon enough.

NARRATOR: It wasn't that Lugalbanda's brothers were cruel. Just the opposite. They were just older—and sometimes older means different. As for Lugalbanda's father, he was so busy pleasing his goddess that he hardly noticed his youngest son.

When Inanna was angry, storm clouds would gather around the top of her towering temple. (*rumbling thunder*) One day it was particularly stormy.

INANNA: (*yelling*) Enmerkar! I am no longer satisfied with this so-called temple. You people must not truly love me!

ENMERKAR: But, my goddess! We do! We do!

INANNA: I'll have you know the King of Aratta has offered me an even more lavish temple than this piddly one I have here!

ENMERKAR: (*gasp*) What? You would really leave me?

INANNA: Let's just say I'm keeping my options open! The city of Aratta is carved from precious stones and adorned with lapis lazuli. I just adore lapis lazuli. It's so blue and shiny.

ENMERKAR: It's settled then! I will conquer the city of Aratta and bring its riches back to Uruk! (*pause*) That would make you happy, wouldn't it?

INANNA: It would make me less unhappy—that's for sure. What are you waiting for? Shoo. Shoo. I'll be waiting here. Hurry back.

NARRATOR: Word went around that Enmerkar's army would soon be marching out, and this news thrilled Lugalbanda.

LUGALBANDA: Now is my time! My brothers have always said when I'm older I can go. Well, I'm older now.

NARRATOR: But Lugalbanda's brothers were not so sure.

BROTHER THREE: War is for men, and you are not a man yet. It is safer for you to stay home.

LUGALBANDA: And miss the war of a lifetime?

BROTHER FOUR: We have seen plenty of war, little brother. Put it off as long as you can.

BROTHER FIVE: Besides the city of Aratta lies on the other side of the deadly Zabu Mountains.

BROTHER SIX: Those mountains are filled with the most frightening monsters known to man.

LUGALBANDA: Ha! Those are stories adults tell to scare children. I'm not afraid!

BROTHER SEVEN: Oh, really? Have you heard of Gud-alim, the beast with the body of a bison and the head of a man?

LUGALBANDA: Sounds ridiculous.

BROTHER ONE: Or creatures with the top-half of a man and the stinging tail of a scorpion.

LUGALBANDA: Kid stuff.

BROTHER TWO: They say even the demon-beast Anzu lives there.

NARRATOR: Everyone had heard of Anzu. The king of the monsters they called him.

LUGALBANDA: I know I'm young, but just give me a chance to prove myself!

NARRATOR: The brothers looked to one another and sighed. Lugalbanda *was* getting older. So they took him before their father for his permission.

BROTHER THREE: Father, Lugalbanda wishes to go to war with us.

ENMERKAR: Lugalbanda? Which one is he? Oh, yes, the little one! It's so hard to keep up with you all. What possessed me to have seven sons?

BROTHER FOUR: Eight, Father.

ENMERKAR: Oh, yes. No wonder your mother died. Parenting is so hard.

BROTHER FIVE: We thought you might be hesitant to send him off to war at such a young age.

ENMERKAR: I don't have time to be worried about *him*. If we don't keep Inanna happy, this whole place will be down the drain. Now hurry and prepare the troops. Tomorrow we depart for Aratta! We will bring its treasures home to add to my glory!

(thunderous booming)

ENMERKAR: I mean, the glory of Inanna, of course! Heh heh!

NARRATOR: As the king rushed off to pacify the goddess, the brothers laughed to one another.

BROTHER SIX: Our father is a slave to that goddess of his.

BROTHER SEVEN: It's a good thing we are such good warriors, or we might resent these missions she sends him on.

BROTHER ONE: Well, Lugalbanda, it looks like you will get to go to war after all.

BROTHER TWO: You are welcome to travel with the troops, but you cannot be in battle.

LUGALBANDA: Fair enough. *(to himself)* We'll see about that.

NARRATOR: It was finally happening. Lugalbanda was so excited he could not sleep at all that night. The next morning, his brothers gave him a spear and outfitted him in some of their old armor.

BROTHER THREE: It's still too big on you.

LUGALBANDA: Who knows? Maybe I will grow into it before we reach Aratta.

NARRATOR: The enormous army of the king was mustered before the city gates. The troops swarmed like a dust cloud, and Lugalbanda loved every minute of it: the flashing armor, the stamping feet, the brandished spears. His brothers led the troops out with grace and dignity.

LUGALBANDA: This is the best day of my life!

NARRATOR: Standing upon the city walls, King Enmerkar addressed his troops.

ENMERKAR: Men, I would like to speak a few words before we depart. Today is a momentous day.

NARRATOR: But just then thunder came rumbling down from the top of Inanna's temple. *(rolling of thunder)*

INANNA: *(booming)* I'm not getting any younger!

ENMERKAR: Yes, my goddess! *(grumbling)* Impossible woman! I don't even get to make an inspirational speech. *(grumble, grumble)*

NARRATOR: The spirits of the soldiers were high as they departed Uruk, but three days later, they neared the Zabu Mountains, which all the men knew were home to monsters.

ENMERKAR: Courage, men! I know these mountains are filled with man-eating monsters that could flay the flesh from your bones…or incinerate you with their fiery breath…or suck out your soul…

BROTHER FOUR: Father!

ENMERKAR: Oh right! But remember, men. Through these mountains is the only way to Aratta, whose city is so heavily fortified it will take us weeks—no months to break through—with heavy casualties…

BROTHER FIVE: Father!

ENMERKAR: But remember the noble cause for which we fight! The glory of our beloved goddess! *(sigh)*

NARRATOR: As they headed into the foreboding mountains, Lugalbanda's brothers warned him again.

BROTHER SIX: Pay extra care as we enter the mountains. They are cursed.

LUGALBANDA: I will fear nothing—just like you, my brothers.

BROTHER SEVEN: Fear and respect are two different things. These mountains are the home of Anzu, the king of demon-beasts. The gods once entrusted him to guard the Tablet of Destinies, but he stole it for himself. It took a great hero to defeat him and win the Tablet back. Then the gods banished him into these mountains, and evil monsters of all kind are drawn to him.

NARRATOR: It seemed that as they climbed higher into the mountains a perceptible gloom hung in the air. Mist covered the ground, and only foul-looking vegetation grew there. Then all of a sudden, a shadow passed over the sun.

BROTHER ONE: Get down!

NARRATOR: Something large and black was soaring overhead—its long tail extended behind it.

BROTHER TWO: *(whispering)* Anzu.

NARRATOR: When the shadow had passed, the troops resumed their climb.

Ever since they had entered the mountains, Lugalbanda had not felt well. He told himself it was just nerves, but his mouth was dry, and his stomach cramped.

LUGALBANDA: Not now. This is my first mission.

NARRATOR: Soon sweat poured from his brow, and he was forced to lean against a rock to catch his breath.

BROTHER THREE: What is it?

LUGALBANDA: Nothing. Nothing.

NARRATOR: He waved his brothers off and pressed on, but then after taking just a few more steps, he collapsed.

BROTHER ONE: Brothers, come quickly!

NARRATOR: His brothers realized a deadly sickness had taken Lugalbanda. His forehead was searing hot, and his eyes are cloudy.

ENMERKAR: What is the matter? We can't halt the army just for a boy—especially not in these evil hills.

BROTHER TWO: Father, he is sick!

ENMERKAR: I realize that, but Inanna will *kill me* if I don't conquer Aratta soon!

NARRATOR: The brothers carried Lugalbanda into one of the caves that dotted the bleak landscape and dabbed his forehead with a damp rag. The seven fearsome warriors became as tender as nursemaids as they cared for their brother.

BROTHER THREE: What can we do? We cannot take him back home. He is too sick to travel.

LUGALBANDA: I'm sorry. I'm so sorry.

NARRATOR: The army halted its progress for a whole day as the brothers tended Lugalbanda. In spite of their care, he seemed to be slipping away from the land of the living.

BROTHER FOUR: I'm afraid he will soon die.

BROTHER FIVE: This is all our fault. We should have never let him come! He *was* too young.

NARRATOR: Lugalbanda was unresponsive, and his breaths grew shallower and shallower.

BROTHER SIX: We are putting the whole army at risk if we stay here any longer. We must move on.

BROTHER SEVEN: You mean, leave Lugalbanda behind?

BROTHER ONE: Either the gods will save him—or they will take him on to the next life.

NARRATOR: They shed tears as they left their brother behind. But just in case he survived, they left him provisions—meat, cheese, bread, butter, hardboiled eggs, water, and wine. They also left him with a dagger of iron and an axe of tin. Then the army marched away, leaving Lugalbanda alone upon the mountain of monsters.

Lugalbanda lay as dead in the cool mountain cave for two whole days. Then on the night of the third, he awoke in a cold sweat.

LUGALBANDA: *(weakly)* Brothers?

NARRATOR: The boy realized he was all alone. Fear and darkness surrounded him. But he was so weak that he could not rise—even if he wanted to. So the boy did all he knew to do.

LUGALBANDA: Shamash, god of the sun, heal me. Let me see your rays once again.

NARRATOR: The last rays of the sun were just leaving the sky, but the sun god Shamash heard the boy and kept him from dying. Faraway, Lugalbanda saw the evening star forming in the sky. It was the form of Inanna.

LUGALBANDA: Inanna, Shamash has spared my life. Please return my strength to me.

NARRATOR: The star seemed to twinkle at him. Then the moon rose.

LUGALBANDA: Nana, goddess of the moon, keep me warm tonight in this strange place.

NARRATOR: And the goddess did. The next morning, Lugalbanda found the strength to rise, and he discovered the provisions his brothers had left for him.

LUGALBANDA: I will return to them! But first I must make it through these deadly mountains.

NARRATOR: Lugalbanda departed the cave and struggled through the mountains. Once again night began to fall, and fear and hunger seized him.

LUGALBANDA: Stay calm. What would my brothers do?

NARRATOR: He struck flint and made a fire. He heated a rock and then warmed his bread upon it. Yellow eyes appeared in the darkness, and he heard faraway howling. *(howling of beasts)* But the fire kept the beasts at bay.

The next day as Lugalbanda picked his way among the rocky peaks like a wild horse, he suddenly froze. A monster was blocking the path ahead. It was a creature with the bottom half of a lion and the top half of a man with an amused smile on his face.

LUGALBANDA: *(gasp)* A monster!

URMAHLULLU: Hey! Words are hurtful, you know.

LUGALBANDA: What do you want from me?

URMAHLULLU: Isn't it obvious? I want what all monsters want. I want to eat you. I saw those bigger humans left you behind. I thought I'd wait around and pick you off after they left.

LUGALBANDA: What are you? A man-cat? A cat-man?

URMAHLULLU: I'm an Urmahlullu. Very deadly.

NARRATOR: The monster lowered itself onto its haunches and crossed its paws.

LUGALBANDA: My brothers left me here. They thought I was—

URMAHLULLU: I'm going to stop you right there. It's not good to get too friendly with your food. It makes me feel conflicted.

LUGALBANDA: But you started a conversation.

URMAHLULLU: I thought maybe you would beg for mercy or something. It helps my self-esteem.

LUGALBANDA: I apologize, Urmah.

URMAHLULLU: Don't call me that. It sounds so girly.

LUGALBANDA: Okay. How about Lullu?

URMAHLULLU: Urmah it is. *(pause)* Hmmm. You don't seem very frightened of me.

LUGALBANDA: Well, when you've glimpsed Anzu, every other monster pales in comparison.

NARRATOR: At the mention of Anzu, the Urmahlullu jumped up and stared at the sky.

URMAHLULLU: Shhh! Are you crazy? No one around here says that name!

LUGALBANDA: Why?

URMAHLULLU: Because…that creature is the head honcho around here. No one messes with him.

LUGALBANDA: Ah. Everyone's afraid of him because he's the monster who stole the Tablet of Destinies from the gods?

URMAHLULLU: Yeah, and when he did, they banished him here. And is he ever cranky about it!

LUGALBANDA: So he has all of you second-rate monsters living in fear.

NARRATOR: The Urmahlullu flicked out its claws.

URMAHLULLU: Grrr. All right. Enough chit-chat. Time for dinner.

LUGALBANDA: *(yelling)* Anzu! Anzu!

URMAHLULLU: Shhhh! Shhh! Do you want to get us both killed? His home is close to here.

LUGALBANDA: I guess I'd rather be eaten by a *real* monster instead of you.

URMAHLULLU: Fine! Fine! I'll leave you alone! Sheesh. It's not like it's personal or anything. It's just the food chain.

NARRATOR: The Urmahlullu slunk away, and Lugalbanda continued higher in the mountains. Soon he saw an amazing sight. On the peak ahead towered an enormous tree. Its massive roots ran down through the rock on every side, and only the Evening Star could have been higher in the sky than its branches.

LUGALBANDA: That must be Anzu's home.

NARRATOR: From the heights of this massive tree, Lugalbanda heard an earth-shaking shriek. *(demonic cawing)*

LUGALBANDA: It is Anzu!

NARRATOR: Then he saw the creature take flight. It had the enormous body of a bird and the head of a lion. Its mouth was filled with a thousand, shark-like teeth. Lugalbanda stared up at it in awe. His body told him to run, his mind told him to hide, but his courage told him to stand his ground. The creature did not spy him and soared away into the distance.

LUGALBANDA: I'll be far away before he returns.

NARRATOR: But as Lugalbanda continued onward, he heard a feeble cry.

CHICK: Raar-cheep!

NARRATOR: Fallen among the rocks was a little chick with the head of a lion cub. Its little bird body was bruised.

LUGALBANDA: It is Anzu's chick. It must have fallen from its high nest.

NARRATOR: When the chick-cub saw Lugalbanda, it turned and hissed.

CHICK: (hissing)

NARRATOR: Lugalbanda took a timid step toward the chick-cub.

URMAHLULLU: I wouldn't do that if I were you.

NARRATOR: Looking up in shock, Lugalbanda saw the Urmahlullu reclining on a nearby boulder.

LUGALBANDA: You again? This is one of Anzu's chicks. It has tried to fly on its own and landed here. It's lost.

URMAHLULLU: Exactly. That's why you just keep walking.

LUGALBANDA: But it looks hurt. It'll die out here.

URMAHLULLU: What do you care? (mockingly) It's a monster.

LUGALBANDA: It may be a monster, but it's still worthy of mercy.

URMAHLULLU: I know. That's why I was going to carry it off and eat it before anyone finds it.

LUGALBANDA: Do you always pick off the smallest and weakest? You're horrible.

URMAHLULLU: Yeah, what part of "monster" is confusing to you?

NARRATOR: Lugalbanda stepped toward the chick-cub, his hands outstretched to show the chick he meant no harm.

LUGALBANDA: Hey, little guy. I know what it's like to be so far away from home.

URMAHLULLU: Oh brother. What are you going to do? Reunite that thing with its Mommy and Daddy? Then to thank you, they'll rip you to shreds.

LUGALBANDA: So what? It is the right thing to do.

URMAHLULLU: (laugh) A noble, little human.

NARRATOR: The Anzu cub did not want Lugalbanda to touch it, but he tempted it with a bit of meat. It gobbled down the meat greedily and then began to lick his hand for more.

LUGALBANDA: Now you like me, don't you?

NARRATOR: He tied his cloak into a sling and placed the chick-cub inside. Then he headed for the massive root of the towering tree.

URMAHLULLU: *(musically)* They're going to kill you! You might as well stay here and let me eat you.

LUGALBANDA: We'll see.

URMAHLULLU: That creature is a thief who stole from the gods. Do you think he'll have mercy on you?

LUGALBANDA: Maybe he learned his lesson.

URMAHLULLU: Monsters don't learn lessons. Crazy human. This I have to see!

NARRATOR: Lugalbanda reached the tree's trunk and started to climb.

LUGALBANDA: Don't worry, little guy. I'll have you home soon.

NARRATOR: The height of the tree made Lugalbanda dizzy, but he continued his climb. At last he reached the nest and snuggled the chick-cub into the branches of juniper and pine he found there. He wrapped his cloak around the baby creature and turned to leave, but just then he heard the concussive cry of Anzu. *(bird screech)* There was nowhere to hide. The bird-beast settled down into the nest with massive swoops of its wings. The lion-like face glared down at Lugalbanda.

ANZU: *(angrily)* Son of the earth, how dare you come to my nest!

NARRATOR: Lugalbanda knew that it would be death to appear afraid, so he did not quail or quiver. He merely bowed his head in respect.

LUGALBANDA: Mighty Anzu, I am Lugalbanda, son of King Enmerkar. I am at your service.

NARRATOR: Anzu opened his mouth wide—exposing row upon row of teeth prepared to bite.

CHICK: Raar-cheep!

NARRATOR: Anzu saw his chick-cub within the nest—tidily tucked back into his place.

ANZU: How did—? *(pause)* Did you find my chick-cub, little prince?

LUGALBANDA: I did, sky-lord. I know what it's like to be lost and alone. That's why I'm here on your mountain. My father and my brothers are traveling to the city of Aratta, but they were forced to leave me behind.

ANZU: Is that so? And you chose to have mercy on my chick-cub—although it is a monster.

LUGALBANDA: Every creature deserves respect.

ANZU: Hmmm. Wise. Well, I have decided. I will not destroy you. In fact, I must give you a gift for saving my chick-cub. I have all the powers of a god, you know. So what will it be—fame, riches, all-consuming power?

LUGALBANDA: No thank you. I do not need any of that.

ANZU: Good answer. That was actually a test. All of those things will only bring you heartache. I should know. I stole the Tablet of Destinies from the gods and because of that, I have been banished here—living in these desolate mountains with my fellow monsters.

LUGALBANDA: So I've heard. All I really want is to be able to help my brothers.

ANZU: Then I shall give you what you need most—speed. I will give you the power to run like the wind.

LUGALBANDA: Really? How wonderful!

ANZU: But you must keep this skill a secret. Tell no one you have it, or it will leave you.

LUGALBANDA: I won't.

ANZU: Your brothers and their warriors are having a trying time taking the city of Aratta. The walls of that city are high, and the people there are brave warriors. Not to mention, the monsters of these mountains have been attacking your brothers and their troops.

LUGALBANDA: Oh no!

ANZU: But you can go to them, and I am certain you can help them, little prince. Today you have taught me a lesson—even the smallest of people can do mighty things.

NARRATOR: Lugalbanda bowed before the colossal creature. As he turned to go, the chick-cub came forward to nuzzle up against him one last time.

ANZU: Farewell, little prince.

NARRATOR: Anzu summoned a breeze, which carried Lugalbanda gently back down toward the earth. As the boy descended toward the base of the tree, he saw the Urmahlullu standing before a group of his fellow monsters—a scorpion woman, a six-headed ram, and a bison with the head of man.

URMAHLULLU: Look, yak-breath, I'm telling you the truth! This human kid just picked up the chick and headed up the tree. Ten to one, Anzu's feeding him to his chick right now.

NARRATOR: Lugalbanda alighted on the ground.

LUGALBANDA: I have returned!

URMAHLULLU: *(fright)* Ah! Oh, human, you're back! So I see his feathered majesty decided *not* to kill you. Good news. That means *we* can eat you now.

LUGALBANDA: Wrong again.

URMAHLULLU: Oh really? *(roaring)* Raar!

NARRATOR: The four monsters lunged for the boy, but Lugalbanda kicked his feet into motion, and he sped away with all the blazing speed of the wind.

URMAHLULLU: Huh. The little booger has some speed on him, doesn't he?

NARRATOR: As Lugalbanda sped through the mountains, many monsters sprang out to end his life, but he passed them all in the blink of an eye. Finally, he reached the far side of the mountains, and the city of Aratta appeared in the valley—his father's army surrounding it. The sight of the city glittering with blue stone took Lugalbanda's breath away.

LUGALBANDA: It really is beautiful!

NARRATOR: When Lugalbanda appeared within the war camp, his brothers couldn't believe it.

BROTHER TWO: Little brother, you survived!

BROTHER THREE: How did you ever make it past all those monsters? We had to fight our way through.

LUGALBANDA: I guess when you're little, the big things of the world pay you no mind. How is the battle going?

BROTHER FOUR: Not good, I'm afraid. The people of Aratta are safe behind their walls. Plus, Inanna has removed her support from the battle. She is furious the war is taking so long. Father is going to send a messenger back to Uruk to beg her to help us.

LUGALBANDA: Let *me* go!

BROTHER FIVE: You? It's too dangerous.

LUGALBANDA: Please! I know I can do it. I will be fast, and I will be back before you know it.

BROTHER SIX: The troops are failing. We won't last much longer.

LUGALBANDA: Trust me, brothers. I can do it.

NARRATOR: The brothers conversed with one another.

BROTHER SEVEN: Well, he did survive in the mountains of the monsters. Maybe he *can* do it.

NARRATOR: So they agreed to give Lugalbanda a chance. He walked out of camp at a normal speed, but once he was out of their sight, he sped away. Back over the mountains he raced, all the way to the tall temple of Uruk. He found the goddess Inanna lounging upon her throne.

INANNA: Who are you and what are you doing here?

LUGALBANDA: I am Lugalbanda. King Enmerkar needs your help!

INANNA: Lugal-what-now?

LUGALBANDA: I am the youngest prince of Uruk. I prayed to you, and you saved my life.

INANNA: Oh yes. The little one.

LUGALBANDA: It was a great act of mercy—especially for a goddess such as you.

INANNA: Hey, I'm demanding, not heartless.

LUGALBANDA: I have come to tell you my father's troops will fail if you don't give them your aid.

INANNA: Well, good! I'm irritated! I wanted that city destroyed by now. It's taking forever!

LUGALBANDA: Is there not a better way? Does Aratta have to be destroyed?

INANNA: How else would I get my precious jewels?

LUGALBANDA: Couldn't you trade?

INANNA: You're not suggesting I share, are you? I'm not so big on sharing.

LUGALBANDA: Uruk already honors you as its goddess, but if you spared Aratta and made them Uruk's ally, they would honor you, too. That's double the glory!

NARRATOR: The goddess's eyes flashed.

INANNA: Two cities to honor me? Why didn't I think of that? In fact, let's just say I *did* think of that. What a smart goddess I am!

LUGALBANDA: So you'll help my father and his army?

INANNA: *(bored-like)* Fine! Tell them they must fish in the river near Aratta for a sacred fish. If they eat of its meat, it will give them the strength to defeat Aratta. I'll tell you how to craft a magic bucket that will catch the fish. *(yawn)*

LUGALBANDA: Wonderful!

INANNA: But listen! Tell the king he must not destroy Aratta. And make sure you tell them it was all my idea to spare it—because it was.

LUGALBANDA: Of course!

NARRATOR: Lugalbanda raced back to Aratta and delivered this message. Once the troops had eaten of the magical fish, they gained incredible strength. The city of Aratta was defeated, but not destroyed. Trade was established between Aratta and Uruk—and more importantly peace.

BROTHER ONE: You have saved the day, little brother!

(cheering from the soldiers)

NARRATOR: As the army marched home in triumph, Lugalbanda looked heavenward. Against the brightness of the sky, he saw the flying form of Anzu followed by the shadow of its chick.

DISCUSSION QUESTIONS

1. Lugalbanda literally means "little prince." Why is it sometimes hard to be the youngest?
2. Were Lugalbanda's brothers wrong to leave him alone in the mountains? Explain.
3. How is Lugalbanda compassionate?
4. If you found a baby monster, would you take pity on it? Explain.
5. According to some sources, King Enmerkar was the first Sumerian ruler to use cuneiform or "wedge writing." He probably ruled around 3,400-3,100 B.C. The story of Lugalbanda, written in cuneiform, was found carved on a stone slab. Scholars theorize this story was written around 2,100-2,000 B.C., making it the oldest written story known to man. Although the story is ancient, how can we still relate to it?
6. Lugalbanda later becomes the king of Uruk and the father of the mighty hero, Gilgamesh. What are some qualities of Lugalbanda that would make him a good king?
7. The demon-monster Anzu was said to breathe fire and was so enormous that the flapping of his wings brought about huge storms. Anzu was so powerful the gods gave him the job of protecting the Tablet of Destinies, which gave infinite power to whomever possessed it. But instead of protecting the Tablet, Anzu stole it for himself, and the archer god,

Ninurta, fought him to reclaim it. Some stories claim Anzu died, but in this story the creature lives in exile in the Zabu Mountains. Based on his interactions with Lugalbanda, has Anzu learned from his past actions? Explain.
8. How are peace and compassion themes in the story?

LI CHI AND THE SERPENT
TEACHER GUIDE

BACKGROUND

Ancient Chinese society was built on the Confucian belief system, established by the Chinese philosopher Confucius (551-479 B.C.). The ultimate goal of Confucianism was to build a strong society by strengthening moral character and the family unit. For this reason, loyalty to the family and respect toward parents was imperative. Families even venerated their deceased ancestors, whom they believed lived on in spirit form. Since this ancestor worship focused on male ancestors only, families prized sons over daughters.

In Confucian thought, men and women were just one example of the complimentary forces of nature: yin and yang, sun and moon, light and darkness. Men's virtues were strength and rigidity while a woman's virtues were respect and compliance. Girls and women were to behave passively toward their male relatives. First, girls were expected to bend to the will of their father (the undisputed master of the household), then their husbands, and eventually their own sons. Their household duties were to rear children, weave, and cook. Although few women worked outside the home, some poor women earned a living by the humble profession of sorcery.

Interestingly, this same culture that undervalued women produced the story of Li Chi, a girl who subverts the conventions of her society, and by doing so, saves her people.

SUMMARY

Shortly after terrorizing the countryside, a giant serpent from the mountains contacts a soothsayer in the capital city of the province through psychic visions. The serpent agrees to cause no more trouble if the people will offer it a yearly sacrifice: a maiden between the ages of twelve and thirteen. The magistrate of the province agrees to this, and makes the Serpent's Soothsayer his royal advisor.

Nine years pass, and nine maidens pay with their lives. Meanwhile, the Soothsayer grows more powerful—extorting bribes from the wealthy families of the province to keep her from choosing their daughters.

In the capital city, a wealthy man named Li Tan is the father of six daughters. His youngest daughter, Chi, does not enjoy traditional female duties and instead dreams of being a warrior. One day after hearing a dog barking in the city street, she begs her father to allow her to adopt it. She names it Huan, which means "happiness," and it becomes her faithful companion.

When Chi finally learns of the yearly sacrifices, she asks her father why the people of the province allow this evil to go on. She vows she would fight the Serpent if allowed. The Soothsayer arrives at Li Tan's home to extort her yearly bribe, but Chi insults her. Li Tan is able to pacify the Soothsayer, but Chi realizes she must end the sacrifices. Taking her father's sword, Chi travels to the magistrate's palace and vows to be the yearly sacrifice. The Soothsayer is delighted at this proposal since Chi has insulted her. The guards bind Chi, transport her into the mountains, and leave her before the Serpent's cave. Huan arrives and chews through Chi's bonds. She fights the snake and slays it after distracting it with a batch of sticky rice balls she has brought along.

32   Hero Tales from World Mythology

Inside the monster's cave, she finds the skulls of the nine girls previously sacrificed.

When she returns to the magistrate, he tells her that when the Serpent died, the Soothsayer's mind left her. Chi has saved the girls of her kingdom from further death. When the king of the realm hears of Chi's bravery, he asks to be her husband and makes Li Tan the new magistrate of the province.

ESSENTIAL QUESTIONS

- Why must we always oppose evil?
- How can young people make an impact when they stand up for what is right?

ANTICIPATORY QUESTION

- Whose job is it to stand up for what is right?

NAME PRONUNCIATIONS

Li Chi	LĒ CHĒ
Li Tan	LĒ TAHN
She Zhu	SHĒ CHOO
Huan	HWAHN
Yung	YOONG

CREATURE FEATURE

The Serpent In Chinese mythology dragons are benevolent guardians of nature, but giant serpents are symbols of evil. Ancient Chinese culture taught that if a ruler was following the teachings of Confucianism correctly, his rule would be peaceful and serene. Therefore, the presence of the Serpent in this story symbolizes the corruption of the province's ruler, and Li Chi's slaying of the monster symbolically heals the land.

TEACHABLE TERMS

- **Metaphor** On pg. 33 the Serpent is described as a "river" of scales.
- **Theme: The opposition of evil** On pg. 34 the narrator states that "if left unchecked, evil will continue to grow and grow." The Serpent symbolizes this idea.
- **Treatment of Women** Ancient Chinese culture considered women to be of lesser worth than men, yet Chi struggles to prove her worth. Comments such as those of the Soothsayer on pg. 35 and Li Tan's defense of his six daughters also on pg. 35 are examples of this.
- **Confucianism** On pg. 36 Chi's father explains to her the complimentary forces of yin and yang central to Confucianism.
- **Connect** The Chinese legend of Mulan features a protagonist similar to Li Chi: Mulan must circumvent her society's gender norms by dressing as a man and joining the army to save the life of her father.

RECALL QUESTIONS

1. What do the people of the province do each year on the eighth day of the eighth month?
2. Who or what does Li Chi find wandering the city streets?
3. What does the Soothsayer want from Li Tan?
4. What does Li Chi use to distract the Serpent?
5. What does Li Chi find in the cavern of the Serpent?

LI CHI AND THE SERPENT

CAST

CHI	*Young Maiden*
FATHER	*Father of Chi*
MOTHER	*Mother of Chi*
SERPENT	*Enormous Monster*
SOOTHSAYER	*Greedy Official*
MAGISTRATE	*Ruler of the Province*
SISTER ONE	*Sister of Chi*
SISTER TWO	*Sister of Chi*
SISTER THREE	*Sister of Chi*
FARMER ONE	*Poor Fieldworker*
FARMER TWO	*Poor Fieldworker*

NARRATOR: It was the sheep that vanished from the fields first—followed by the oxen. When the farmers near the Yung Mountains discovered their livestock disappearing bit by bit, they suspected thieves, but when they found wide, trough-like tracks left in the mud, they realized they had a much bigger problem.

FARMER ONE: What could have left these? A dragon?

FARMER TWO: Of course not! Dragons are protectors. This must be a serpent—a destroyer! A monster like we have never seen!

NARRATOR: So they set a watch on the edges of the fields—waiting for what they might see by moonlight. Their efforts were rewarded when shortly after midnight, a river of red and gold scales came gliding down the mountain. It was a serpent eighty feet long and as wide as a span of ten hands—an emergent evil.

FARMER ONE: *(cry of shock)* Ancestors protect us!

FARMER TWO: It is even larger than I feared!

NARRATOR: The frightened farmers did not stop running until they reached the capital city, where they demanded an audience with the magistrate, who, rumpled from sleep, greeted them groggily in his official palace.

MAGISTRATE: *(yawn)* This had better be good.

FARMER ONE: We have seen it! A monster from the mountains!

FARMER TWO: A giant snake!

MAGISTRATE: *(sigh)* Deliver me from peasants. *(to them)* You two were probably just dreaming.

FARMER ONE: No! Nothing could be more real! Its head was as big as a barrel, and its eyes were like mirrors!

FARMER TWO: And it was long, too! Several *li* long!

MAGISTRATE: Fine! It's probably nothing more than a garden snake, but I'll send some soldiers to scout it out tomorrow. Now leave me in peace!

NARRATOR: The next morning the magistrate sent a squadron of his best soldiers up into the mountains to search for the monster. To his shock, only one soldier returned alive—and reported the rest devoured.

MAGISTRATE: *(gasp)* Thirty soldiers completely gobbled up? Armor and all? This is going to be a bigger problem than I thought.

NARRATOR: The magistrate declared all paths into the mountains closed. He hoped the problem would just go away. But that is not the nature of evil. Left unchecked, it will continue to grow and grow. Meanwhile, the Serpent had tasted human flesh and craved more.

In the capital city there lived a soothsayer—a poor, ragged woman who earned a few meager coins off reading palms. One night as she slept against the city walls, she had a strange dream. Out of the misty recesses of her mind appeared a pair of yellow eyes—shining like beacons through the darkness.

SERPENT: *(hissing)* Ssserve me. Ssssend me livesss—young livesssss. If you sssserve me, I will make you great.

NARRATOR: The Soothsayer awoke—her body drenched in sweat—and made her way to the palace of the magistrate. The guards ordered her to cease her crazed cries, but when she would not relent, they dragged her before their lord and flung her at his feet.

MAGISTRATE: Can't a man get any sleep around here? *(sigh)* What do you want, you old charlatan?

NARRATOR: The Soothsayer rose and, gathering her tattered robes about her, faced the magistrate imperiously.

SOOTHSAYER: She Zhu, the Almighty Serpent has appeared in my dreams! He swears he will curse the entire kingdom if you don't heed his demands.

MAGISTRATE: Demands? I don't negotiate with reptiles!

NARRATOR: The Soothsayer glided eerily forward, and the unearthly light gleaming in her eyes caused the magistrate to squirm.

SOOTHSAYER: You underestimate his power. He will grow and grow until he devours us all.

MAGISTRATE: What does this…creature request of us?

SOOTHSAYER: She Zhu requests a yearly sacrifice.

MAGISTRATE: *(angrily)* Impossible! I won't offer my people up to a monster!

SOOTHSAYER: So you're willing to sacrifice *your* life to him then?

MAGISTRATE: As you were saying…

SOOTHSAYER: The Almighty One is tired of feasting on tough and chewy men. He craves succulent flesh—female flesh. Each year you must send him a soft maiden between the ages of twelve and thirteen, and he will leave the rest of us in peace.

MAGISTRATE: Oh, is that it? Just young girls? With all that build up, I was expecting something much worse.

SOOTHSAYER: Yes, but even daughters are precious to some. So you must choose carefully. In fact, I propose you let *me* do the choosing for you. Let the people's anger fall on *me*. But for this service, I require… compensation. You must make me your *official* soothsayer.

MAGISTRATE: *(not sure)* Hmmm. You? Living here in the palace? I don't know.

SOOTHSAYER: *(loudly)* If you don't listen to me, She Zhu will destroy us all!

MAGISTRATE: *(sigh)* Very well.

NARRATOR: So the magistrate installed the Soothsayer as his advisor, promising her riches and power.

MAGISTRATE: People of the province, hear me! The Mighty Serpent has spoken! We must pay his price, or we will all perish.

(murmuring of the people)

NARRATOR: The following week, the Soothsayer chose the Serpent's first victim—a daughter of poor laborers. Soldiers bound the girl's hands and feet, carried her into the mountains, and left her helpless before the Serpent's cave. *(girl screaming in fright)* As the soldiers fled for cover, the monster shot out of the shadows, devoured the offering, and slithered back into the darkness.

SERPENT: I have been appeassssed…for a year.

NARRATOR: So began a yearly cycle of suffering and shame. While the people of the province tried to forget the high price they paid for peace, the Soothsayer kept the Serpent ever in their minds. She dressed herself in flowing robes of red and gold—patterned in mimicry of the master she served. She grew fat on bribes, threatening to doom the daughters of the prosperous if they did not give what she demanded.

Nine years passed, and nine innocent girls lost their lives. All knew what an injustice this was, but no one was brave enough to oppose the Soothsayer or her master. They consoled themselves with the fact that the victims were just daughters—and poor daughters at that. It seemed nothing would ever end the Serpent's reign of terror.

In the capital city, there lived a well-respected man named Li Tan, who was blessed in every way—except for one. He had no sons, only six daughters. When the other men of the town teased him about this, he only laughed.

FATHER: *(chuckle)* Do not speak to me of misfortune! I consider my daughters to be my greatest blessings!

NARRATOR: His youngest daughter, the apple of his eye, was named Chi. She was not delicate and refined like his other daughters. In fact, she often shirked her household duties to practice swordsmanship with a crude weapon she had carved herself.

MOTHER: *(angrily)* Chi! Come here at once!

NARRATOR: One day, Chi was summoned to the household kitchen, where her mother and sisters were preparing the evening meal. She bowed to her mother, carefully hiding her wooden sword behind her back.

CHI: Yes, Mother?

MOTHER: Ha! Don't even pretend to respect me! While you have been playing silly games, your sisters and I have been busy doing the day's work! Now sit!

NARRATOR: Chi sulkily seated herself at the table where her older sisters eyed her coldly.

SISTER ONE: *(snidely)* Well, if it isn't our little sister, the swordfighter!

SISTER TWO: She needs to be a warrior. The only way she'll ever win a husband is if she beats him into submission.

SISTER THREE: She definitely won't win one with her cooking!

CHI: Maybe I want a husband who will love me for something other than my cooking skills.

MOTHER: Shhh! You will cook for your husband! You will weave! You will be gracious and compliant. A good daughter brings honor to the family—not disgrace.

NARRATOR: Chi's mother slammed a bowl of rice down before her.

MOTHER: *Our* work is done. Now we'll leave you to yours.

NARRATOR: As Chi's mother and her sisters left her alone in the kitchen, she began to prepare the rice and halfheartedly form it into balls. But it was not long until she put this work aside and pulled out her wooden sword. She had crafted it to be the exact size of her father's, which hung in a place of honor in the family shrine.

CHI: *(sigh)* If only I could fight for a living. Cooking is such a worthless skill.

FATHER: *Worthless* is a strong word.

NARRATOR: Her father was standing in the kitchen entryway—watching her with an amused smile.

CHI: Oh, Father! I didn't see you there!

NARRATOR: Chi rose and bowed to him.

FATHER: Sit. Sit. Don't let me interrupt what you are doing. *(pause)* What *are* you doing anyway?

CHI: Failing.

NARRATOR: She held up one of the lopsided rice balls she had formed.

CHI: I am no good at the things Mother wants me to do. All these tasks seem so pointless to me. Why can I not practice with your sword instead? I am good at that!

FATHER: It is not the way of the world, Chi. Men are strong, and women are yielding. It is a balance between the sun and moon, light and shadow, yin and yang. It takes both to make the whole. *(pause)* Now let's see how you have done.

NARRATOR: He took a bite of one of the rice balls.

FATHER: (*unconvincingly*) Mmmmm.

CHI: (*hopefully*) Is it good?

FATHER: (*with a full mouth*) Chewy. Definitely chewy.

NARRATOR: With effort, he swallowed the bite. (*sound of belabored gulping*)

FATHER: Chi, I will *always* be proud of you…even if you are not the best cook.

CHI: (*sadly*) I will try harder, Father! I want to prove myself. I am just so…worthless.

FATHER: There's that word again. Chi, no one is worthless who brings joy to another. And you bring me great joy. Now show me a smile.

NARRATOR: Chi's father lifted her chin, and a smile spread across her face.

FATHER: That's better.

(*distant whimpering of a dog*)

CHI: (*in shock*) Do you hear that?

NARRATOR: Chi ran to the gate of their home and flung it open. In the street outside she saw a dog shivering in the mud. Without hesitation, she scooped it up, and it eagerly licked her face. She returned to her father with it in her arms.

CHI: Father! Look! Can we keep it?

FATHER: A dog? Dogs are for country laborers and farmers. They have no use here.

CHI: But you just told me that nothing is worthless if it brings joy to another.

FATHER: Chi…

CHI: Please, Father! Maybe he just needs a chance to prove his worth—like me!

NARRATOR: Her father smiled knowingly.

FATHER: (*laugh*) Very well. Feed it some of your cooking. That will keep him quiet!

NARRATOR: So the dog, which Chi named Huan or "happiness," came to live with the family, and he did fill Chi's days with newfound joy.

Yet, unbeknownst to Chi, a yearly pall was falling over the province. The eighth month was nearing, when the Soothsayer began her annual rounds—traveling from town to town to squeeze bribes from those who could afford to pay them.

One day Chi overheard her sisters discussing this in hushed tones.

SISTER ONE: It is the eighth month again. That horrible Soothsayer will be here soon to collect her bribe.

SISTER TWO: She asks more and more every year. What if Father and Mother cannot pay? She might choose one of us out of spite.

CHI: Choose you for what?

SISTER THREE: Shh! Not in front of Chi. She's too young to know!

CHI: Too young to know what?

NARRATOR: After much begging, Chi's older sisters finally told her of the yearly sacrifice.

CHI: I can't believe it! Why would our people allow such a thing to happen?

SISTER ONE: Don't worry. I'm sure Father will be able to pay her price.

CHI: But what about girls whose fathers cannot pay?

SISTER TWO: That is not our problem.

CHI: This is *everyone's* problem. Why doesn't someone just slay the Serpent?

SISTER THREE: Oh, and who would do that? You?

SISTER ONE: The Serpent is a hundred feet long! It would take more than that toothpick you play with to slay it!

CHI: I could do it—if I was given a chance.

SISTER TWO: Li Chi the warrior! I can see it now!

(laughter of the sisters)

NARRATOR: Tears welled up in Chi's eyes as she searched out her father. She fell into his arms, and her questions came out in a rush of sobs.

CHI: *(through tears)* Father! Is it really true? Are young girls really offered up to a monster?

NARRATOR: Li Tan's face filled with pain.

FATHER: I have always dreaded this day, but I guess now you are finally old enough to know the truth. It is how things must be. If we give the monster just a single life each year, it will leave us in peace. But do not concern yourself. You will never have to be the sacrifice.

CHI: But how can everyone be fine with this? Others are losing their lives—for us.

FATHER: Chi...

CHI: Why don't you do something, Father? Why is everyone being so cowardly? If it were sons being sacrificed, would our people sit idly by?

NARRATOR: Her father rose angrily.

FATHER: *(angrily)* Chi! You must learn your place! I fear I have indulged you too much. You do not understand the ways of the world. Yielding and compliant—these are the qualities of a woman. Leave the strength and courage for the men.

CHI: But what if the men will not do what is right?

FATHER: We cannot fight a man-eating monster!

CHI: You *cannot* do what you *will not* do.

FATHER: Chi! You will not speak so! Now leave me! You have shamed me with your words!

NARRATOR: Chi's father turned his back on her, and she returned to her chambers and flung herself down upon her mat. As she lay there, it seemed she could hear the cries of the sacrificed—calling out for help vainly before the darkness swallowed them.

These reveries were soon interrupted by her mother, who burst into her room out of breath.

MOTHER: What are you doing lying down? Don't you know? The Soothsayer is coming! We must prepare! Find that mutt of yours and tie it up. I won't have it embarrassing us in front of the Soothsayer.

NARRATOR: Soon an entourage entered the gate of Li Tan's home—servants carrying the Soothsayer in an ornate litter. Li Tan and his family were there to greet them, bowing respectfully.

FATHER: You honor us with your presence, Soothsayer.

SOOTHSAYER: Li Tan! You know the purpose of my visit, I assume. I have come to collect your yearly offering. Your contribution last year was…adequate, but this year I expect even more.

FATHER: (*hesitantly*) Even more? Our family is already strained as it is.

SOOTHSAYER: Careful, Li Tan. No one knows where the anger of the mighty Serpent will fall. For your sake, I hope that it does not fall upon your household—so full of daughters…

FATHER: (*slowly*) I understand your meaning.

SOOTHSAYER: Then you agree to pay my price?

NARRATOR: Chi looked up defiantly.

CHI: (*forcefully*) No.

SOOTHSAYER: I'm sorry, but did one of *your daughters* say something to me?

FATHER: No, your excellency.

CHI: (*loudly*) We will pay you nothing, you old vulture!

SOOTHSAYER: (*gasping*) How dare you!

FATHER: Chi! Silence! Forgive her, Soothsayer. She has a fever, and it has affected her mind.

SOOTHSAYER: I have never been so insulted in all my life! Just for that, I'm asking double your normal contribution!

NARRATOR: Just then, Huan burst out of the kitchen, charging at the ankles of the Soothsayer's litterbearers. (*loud barking*) In their shock, the servants sprang backward, spilling the Soothsayer to the ground. (*thudding*)

SOOTHSAYER: (*screaming*) Argh!

NARRATOR: Chi's sisters covered their mouths to suppress their giggles. (*giggling*) The Soothsayer jumped up from the ground, her eyes flaming.

SOOTHSAYER: (*roaring*) Silence!

NARRATOR: Li Tan fell upon his knees before her.

FATHER: Please, your eminence. Take what little we have, and I will find a way to pay the rest—just please accept our humble apology.

SOOTHSAYER: Fine. Pray that I forget this embarrassing display!

NARRATOR: After the Soothsayer had departed in a huff, Li Tan struggled to his feet.

CHI: Father! How could you?

FATHER: How could *you*? If I had not given her what she asked, you would have been given to the Serpent.

CHI: *(crying out)* Better me than someone else's daughter! What good am I? I am nothing. In fact, I am your sixth nothing!

NARRATOR: Chi stormed away and hid herself in her room. She pulled out her wooden sword—and staring at it in contempt—broke it across her knee. *(Snap!)*

CHI: This must end.

NARRATOR: That night when all the household had succumbed to sleep, Chi snuck into the family shrine and slid her father's sword from where it was bracketed to the wall. She strapped it to her body beneath her garments and headed toward the household gate. But as she passed through the kitchen, she paused.

CHI: Maybe just one more weapon.

NARRATOR: As she stole out into the darkened street, Huan appeared at her heels. *(barking of a dog)*

CHI: No, boy! You must stay here. I will do this alone.

NARRATOR: Chi traveled the empty streets all the way to the magistrate's palace. The guards there were surprised to see a young girl rapping on the gates, but when she refused to leave, they led her before the magistrate.

MAGISTRATE: Doesn't anyone visit during the daytime anymore?

SOOTHSAYER: Li girl? What are you doing here?

CHI: I have come to offer myself to the Serpent.

SOOTHSAYER: Ha! I thought perhaps you'd come to apologize for your outlandish behavior!

CHI: I would never apologize to the likes of you. You are even more coldblooded than the master you serve.

MAGISTRATE: *(laughing)* Ouch.

NARRATOR: Chi turned to the magistrate.

CHI: And *you* are no better! Shame on you—offering your people up to a monster.

MAGISTRATE: *(sheepishly)* It was funnier when you said that to her.

SOOTHSAYER: Enough! You will have your request! The Serpent chooses this girl as the sacrifice!

MAGISTRATE: Fine. Fine. Just let me get back to sleep.

NARRATOR: The palace soldiers came forward and bound Chi's wrists and ankles.

CHI: Why must I be bound? I am just a powerless girl. What harm could I do?

SOOTHSAYER: To make sure you do not run when you behold my master.

CHI: I do not fear him.

SOOTHSAYER: Oh, but you will before the end.

NARRATOR: As the soldiers dragged Chi away, the Soothsayer's eyes glowed with an eerie light.

SOOTHSAYER: Master, I am sending you a sacrifice full of fire. Break her!

NARRATOR: The soldiers threw Chi into a rickety cart and carried her up deep into the Yung Mountains, where an ominous cave opened in the cliffside. The soldiers, beside themselves with fright, heaved Chi to the ground and disappeared back down the mountain as quickly as they could.

After they had departed, from the cave came the sound of scales scratching upon rock. *(sliding scales)* Chi frantically struggled against her bonds, but the ropes were too tight.

SERPENT: Sssso, the one with the will ssstrong enough to defy my Ssssoothsayer has finally come to me.

NARRATOR: A pair of eyes, shining like mirrors, appeared in the dark cave mouth. Chi redoubled her efforts to free herself.

CHI: *(grunting)*

SERPENT: Yessss, now you ssseee. There is no esssscape.

(barking of a dog)

NARRATOR: Appearing around the bend of the rocky path, Huan came running.

CHI: Huan! You followed me!

NARRATOR: The dog bit through the ropes that bound Chi's wrists, and with a single, swift motion, she pulled the sword from beneath her robes, cut loose her feet, and spun toward the cave. The Serpent was free of its lair now—its flat head raised fifteen feet into the air—poised to strike. Chi raised her sword.

CHI: I am Li Chi, and I have come to slay you! No more will you enslave my people!

SERPENT: *(deadly hiss)* Bold wordsss from a worthlessss girl!

NARRATOR: Fire flashed in the Serpent's eyes, and it struck at the girl—lightning swift. She was barely able to dodge to the side before the Serpent's fangs pierced the rocky ground. It struck again, but this time Chi's sword flashed out. *(Slash!)*

SERPENT: *(cry of pain)* Gargh!

NARRATOR: The Serpent drew back, and Huan sprang forward—biting into the flesh of the Serpent's back. The Serpent struck at the dog, seizing up his body and flinging him against the nearby cliff. *(cry of pain from the dog)* Huan fell to the ground and lay motionless.

CHI: *(crying out)* No!

NARRATOR: The Serpent whipped its tail toward Chi, but she dashed up the side of a rocky outcropping and, leaping free of the rock, flung herself upon the head of the snake—stabbing downward into one of its eyes.

SERPENT: *(cry of pain)* Rargh!

NARRATOR: Blood spewed from the Serpent's empty socket, but his tail shot out, coiling itself around Chi's body, squeezing the breath from her.

SERPENT: It isss over.

NARRATOR: The Serpent raised the girl up before its fearsome face.

SERPENT: Now you will fear. Now you will sssee what it feelsss like to be devoured…bit by bit.

NARRATOR: Tears welled up in Chi's eyes.

CHI: *(sadly)* What was I thinking? I was so foolish. How could I, a humble girl, contend with your will? Before you take my life, accept this humble offering.

NARRATOR: Chi pulled a bundle from beneath her robe.

SERPENT: I desssire nothing except your young flesssssh.

NARRATOR: She tore open the bundle to reveal a batch of sticky rice balls.

SERPENT: *(sniffing)* What is that ssssmell? Well, maybe just a tassste.

NARRATOR: The Serpent lowered its head to savor their sweetness. This distraction was all that Chi needed.

CHI: Taste my blade, monster!

NARRATOR: Driving her sword upward with all her might, Chi pierced the Serpent's jaw and lodged her blade deep in its brain. The Serpent fell to the ground lifeless, and its coils unclenched. Chi rose triumphantly to survey her slain enemy.

CHI: Hmmm. Perhaps cookery isn't so worthless after all.

NARRATOR: Chi ran to where Huan had fallen and cradled his crumpled body. At her touch, the dog stirred and weakly licked her face.

CHI: Huan! You're alive! I will get you home…but first…

NARRATOR: Chi turned toward the monster's lair. It seemed to be beckoning her. She stepped inside, and as her eyes adjusted to the darkness, she beheld the skulls of nine young girls lining the cave wall.

CHI: *(sadly)* For your timidity you were devoured. If only you had found the strength to be brave.

NARRATOR: With Huan in her arms and her father's sword slung over her shoulder, Li Chi made her way back down the mountain path. When she reappeared in the capital city, the magistrate looked as if he were seeing a ghost.

MAGISTRATE: But…but…you were sacrificed to the Serpent!

NARRATOR: Chi bowed, displaying her sword before her.

CHI: The Serpent is no more. I have slain him.

MAGISTRATE: But you? A girl?

CHI: Now I humbly ask you to banish your corrupt Soothsayer from this land forever.

MAGISTRATE: Funny you should mention that…

NARRATOR: The magistrate led Chi into the palace courtyard, where the Soothsayer sat clucking and flapping her arms among the chickens.

SOOTHSAYER: *(chicken noises)* Cluck! Cluck! Cluck!

NARRATOR: He explained how at the moment of the Serpent's death, her mind had left her—linked to her master's until the bitter end.

CHI: Fitting. *(to the magistrate)* Now do the right thing and return all the goods this evil woman has stolen from our people.

MAGISTRATE: Yes! Most definitely, young lady!

NARRATOR: Then Chi turned her steps toward home. When she was still far off, she saw her father waiting for her, and she ran into his open arms.

FATHER: *(happily)* My daughter! Thank heavens you are all right! All of the province is talking about what you have done!

CHI: Forgive me for defying you, Father. But it was the only way.

FATHER: No, no. Forgive me. You showed the bravery I could not! You have taught your old father a lesson.

CHI: Then I have proved my worth?

FATHER: Of course! Of course! You have brought me more happiness than ten sons ever could have!

NARRATOR: News of Chi's mighty deed spread throughout all the provinces of the kingdom—even reaching the ears of the young king of the realm. In admiration of Chi's bravery, he came to meet her in person and did not leave before asking for her hand in marriage. The king removed the corrupt magistrate and appointed Li Tan in his place. In the end Chi proved how valuable a daughter could be. Because of one girl, the land was once again free from fear.

DISCUSSION QUESTIONS

1. What makes Li Chi a hero?
2. The story states that if left unopposed, evil will continue to grow stronger and stronger. How is this true in the real world?
3. Li Tan tells his daughter, "No one is worthless who brings joy to another." Do you agree with this statement? Explain.
4. Li Chi was forced to prove her own worth to her society. Have you ever felt the need to prove yourself? Explain.
5. In the ancient Chinese belief system of Confucianism, women were expected to be obedient, gentle, and meek. How does Li Chi subvert these expectations?
6. What does this myth have to say about equality between men and women?
7. In Chinese mythology serpents were symbols of evil. What type of evil could the Serpent in this story symbolize?
8. Li Chi proves that even young people can stand up for what is right. In the real world what prevents people from doing the right thing?

MOMOTARO THE PEACH BOY
TEACHER GUIDE

BACKGROUND

Japan has produced many mythical heroes, but probably the most famous (and most interesting) is Momotaro, the peach-boy warrior. Born out of a giant peach, Momotaro goes on an adventure to defeat fearsome monsters called Oni. In Japanese mythology, Oni, sometimes called *demons* or *ogres*, are evil monsters with huge horns and tusks. They are often depicted as humanoid with either bright red or blue skin. The Oni are formidable opponents who fight with iron clubs. There is even a saying "Oni with an iron club" meaning something that is invincible or undefeatable. Even in modern times some Japanese villages hold festivals in the springtime to ward off Oni by throwing soybeans at people dressed in Oni masks and shouting, "Oni out! Luck in!" They also place Oni-faced tiles on the edges of their roofs to drive away any other evil spirits. In some Japanese versions of the game tag, the person who is "it" is referred to as "the Oni" instead.

SUMMARY

Momotaro is born after an elderly woman finds a giant peach bobbing down the river. When she and her husband try to cut open the peach, they find a baby inside. Realizing that the baby has been sent to them from heaven, they name him Momotaro, which means "peach boy," and raise him as their own.

When Momotaro is sixteen years old, news reaches his mother and father that fearsome monsters called Oni have abducted many people from the coastal region and taken them back to their Island-Kingdom. Momotaro vows to rescue these people from the Oni. For a parting gift his mother gives him a bag full of dumplings.

As Momotaro journeys toward the Island-Kingdom of the Oni, he is joined by three animal companions—Inu the dog, Saru the monkey, and Kiji the pheasant. In return for their help, Momotaro gives them each some of his mother's delicious dumplings. When they reach the sea, Momotaro and his animal companions cross over to the Island-Kingdom in a fishing boat. Momotaro sends Kiji up to the Oni mountaintop fortress to cause a diversion while he, Inu, and Saru find a secret way inside.

Momotaro finds a tunnel that leads up through the mountain to the Oni fortress. Inside the tunnel he encounters two maidens, who are prisoners of the Oni, doing their laundry in an underground river. They give him their father's sword, which they managed to bring with them from the mainland.

Once Momotaro and his animal companions reach the Oni fortress, they defeat the Oni. The Oni King begs for his life, and Momotaro agrees to spare him if all the Oni will break off their horns and become kindly spirits who do good to humans. The Oni agree. Momotaro returns home rich from the treasures of the Oni hoard. He builds himself a palace where he, his family, and his new pets live happily ever after.

ESSENTIAL QUESTIONS

- Why is teamwork important?
- How can a variety of skills help when faced with an obstacle?

46 Hero Tales from World Mythology

ANTICIPATORY QUESTIONS

- What are some Asian myths or legends you have heard?
- What are Oni?
- Can you think of a hero who had an unusual birth?

CONNECT

Culture Although the legend of Momotaro has many variants, his story is most associated with the Japanese city of Okayama, which claims to be the home of the hero. In Okayama there is a shrine and a museum dedicated to a prince named Kibitsuhiko-no-mikoto, who many believe is the real-life inspiration for the Momotaro legend. Every year Okayama has a Momotaro festival in the summer. Some festival participants dress up like Oni, and vendors sell dumplings (like those from Momotaro's story) and locally-grown peaches.

NAME PRONUNCIATIONS

Momotaro	MŌ-MŌ-TAH-RŌ
Fii San	FĒ-SAHN
Oni	Ō-NĒ
Inu	Ē-NOO
Saru	SAH-ROO
Kiji	KĒ-JĒ

TEACHABLE TERMS

- **Language** In the original story, Momotaro's animal companions are nameless. In this version of the story they are given the names *Inu*, *Saru*, and *Kiji*, which mean *dog, monkey,* and *pheasant* respectively in the Japanese language. Fii San, the name of Momotaro's father, is also Japanese for *old man.*

- **Metaphor** On pg. 50 Momotaro uses a metaphor comparing his belly to a shameless dog, which is always growling for food. Inu the dog does not appreciate this metaphor.

- **Homophones** On pg. 53 Saru refers to Kiji as "one foul fowl" making a pun on the homophones *foul* and *fowl*.

- **Idiom/Pun** On pg. 53 Kiji the pheasant says, "A little birdie told me," which is an idiom implying that the speaker wants to hide the source of certain information. In this case, it is also a pun since Kiji *is* a bird.

- **Alliteration** On pg. 57 Momotaro uses alliteration when he refers to his enemies as "odious Oni."

- **Pun** On pg. 58 Momotaro makes a pun on the word *pit* meaning both "to set against" and "the center of a peach."

RECALL QUESTIONS

1. What is strange about the way that Momotaro was born?
2. What three creatures help Momotaro on his quest?
3. What are Oni?
4. What special item does Momotaro receive from two maidens?
5. What does Momotaro make the Oni promise?

Momotaro the Peach Boy 47

MOMOTARO THE PEACH BOY

CAST

FII SAN	*Poor, Old Man*
WIFE	*His Wife*
MOMOTARO	*Peach Boy*
INU	*Loyal Dog*
SARU	*Tricky Monkey*
KIJI	*Wise Pheasant*
MAIDEN ONE	*Wealthy Girl*
MAIDEN TWO	*Wealthy Girl*
ONI KING	*Evil Monster Ruler*
ONI	*Evil Monster*
FISHERMAN	*Poor Man*

NARRATOR: Many centuries ago in Japan, there lived a poor, old man, Fii San, and his wife. One day as the wife was washing her clothes by the side of a swift river, she spied something floating down the river. It was large, bulbous, and orange. It was a peach.

WIFE: *(excitedly)* What a large peach! Mmmmm. I'm sure it's tasty, too!

NARRATOR: Dropping her wash, the old woman picked up a stick to retrieve the peach, but it was too far out.

WIFE: Drat! Fii San and I could live on that peach for a month. But how will I reach it?

NARRATOR: Then the old woman remembered a chant her mother had taught her when she was a little girl. She had always wondered if it might be a magic spell.

WIFE: It's worth a shot!
(chanting)
That distant water is bitter,
But the nearer water is better.
Pass that water by, and for a treat
Swim over here into the sweet.

NARRATOR: As if responding to her voice, the peach bobbed over into the shallow water.

WIFE: *(giddy laugh)* Ha! You are all mine now. Tonight Fii San and I shall have a merry meal! *(grunting)* Ugh. This thing is heavier than it looks.

NARRATOR: When the old woman arrived home, her husband was just coming in from the fields.

FII SAN: *(surprised)* Woman, what is that you carry in your arms?

WIFE: *(grunting)* An enormous peach! And my back is killing me. I always thought fruit was healthy for you, but now I'm not so sure. Help me get it inside!

FII SAN: *(angrily)* Wife, how much did that thing cost? We cannot afford it!

WIFE: I did not buy it, old man. I found it! We'll have it for our dinner.

NARRATOR: The old man helped his wife get the peach inside their simple hut.

FII SAN: *(excitedly)* Oooh! It is a fine peach! My mouth is watering already! Let me cut it open.

NARRATOR: Just as Fii San brought a knife close to the peach's finely-haired skin, they heard a strange, muffled noise come from inside the peach. *(child-like laughter)*

WIFE: Did you hear that? Do you think this peach is…haunted?

FII SAN: I don't care! We'll eat it anyway!

NARRATOR: The childlike laughter escaped the peach again, which began to shake and tremble.

FII SAN: *(frightened)* This peach is cursed!

NARRATOR: In that instant the skin of the peach unfurled like a flower's petals. Sitting in the midst of the peelings was a smiling baby boy. *(baby laugh)*

FII SAN: *(angrily)* What? We cannot eat *this*! What kind of trick are you trying to pull on me, wife?

WIFE: Oh, Fii San! Don't you see? This is a gift from the gods—sent to us in our old age!

NARRATOR: The old woman scooped up the baby boy and added her own laughter to his.

WIFE: *(happily)* A child! A child!

FII SAN: *(with a mouthful of peach)* And there's still plenty of peach to eat, too!

WIFE: We shall name him Momotaro because he is our "peach boy"—our little gift from Heaven!

FII SAN: Well, get a diaper on him before he makes a little gift on the table.

NARRATOR: For the next fifteen years Momotaro was the apple—or should we say, peach—of his old parents' eye. Although he never grew as tall as other boys, Momotaro soon became far stronger and far smarter. The neighbors whispered that he would either do something incredible or something horrible—so they avoided him, just to play it safe. One day Fii San returned to their simple hut with a look of distress upon his face.

FII SAN: There is much gossip in the village, wife.

WIFE: Are they spreading rumors about our darling peach-boy again?

FII SAN: No! Up and down the coastline people have been stolen from their homes in the middle of the night. *(whispering)* It is the Oni.

WIFE: Oh my!

FII SAN: They have been dragging their prisoners back to the Island-Kingdom and devouring them one by one. They have attacked ships at sea as well—carrying off any treasures they found there. The governors have sent a petition to the Emperor himself—to send a mighty warrior to defeat the Oni.

WIFE: Impossible! Nothing can defeat the Oni. Oh, those poor people.

NARRATOR: Momotaro had been listening to his parents' conversation with great interest.

MOMOTARO: What are Oni?

FII SAN: Nothing that concerns you, boy. I just pray that they never find their way here.

MOMOTARO: You don't have to hide things from me anymore. Tell me.

WIFE: Oni are huge demon-monsters! They have hideous features and long curved horns—or so it's said! No one lives long enough to get a good look at them.

NARRATOR: Momotaro paused thoughtfully.

MOMOTARO: I must go save these people from such fearsome creatures.

WIFE: No, my son, no!

MOMOTARO: Why not? You said that those people are in trouble.

FII SAN: Not even a great hero could defeat the Oni, I'm afraid. We even have a saying, "As undefeatable as an Oni with an iron club." It's impossible!

MOMOTARO: They only say that because no one has done it before. I want to go and try. My whole life you have told me that I am special. Why would you hold me back now?

WIFE: Because you will be killed! What could you possibly gain from this?

MOMOTARO: I could save those people. And who says that the Oni will not start raiding further inland? Eventually, they will find their way here.

FII SAN: No! I forbid it! No adventures for you, young man!

MOMOTARO: You said the Oni have plundered the ships of passing sailors. They will have a horde of gold. Once I have defeated them, I can bring their treasure back here, and we won't have to be poor anymore.

FII SAN: Oooh. Good point. Off you go!

WIFE: *(angrily)* Fii San!

NARRATOR: Momotaro finally convinced his parents to allow him to go to the Island-Kingdom and fight the demon-like Oni who lived there.

WIFE: Every hero needs something special to help him succeed—a sword or an amulet. But we are so poor that we have nothing to give you...except these.

MOMOTARO: *(laughs)* A bag of rice dumplings! My favorite!

WIFE: At least you will not be starving. Now, kiss me and be on your way.

NARRATOR: Momotaro bade his parents goodbye, setting out on the road that led to the sea. After traveling many miles, the boy found the thought of his mother's dumplings gnawing at his mind—and his stomach. *(growling stomach)* He sat down in the shade of the roadside hedge and brought out the bundled bits.

MOMOTARO: The belly will give you no rest until it is fed. It is a shameless dog.

INU: I don't like what you're implying, bub.

NARRATOR: Momotaro turned his head. A great dog, as big as a pony, had appeared through the hedge. The dog bared its teeth and growled deeply.

INU: *(hatefully)* Hand over the dumplings, and no one gets hurt!

MOMOTARO: Oh, hello.

INU: *(growling)* You don't seem very frightened of me!

MOMOTARO: *(laughing)* Should I be?

INU: Grrrr. How dare you laugh at me, miserable human! I am Inu the Destroyer— and I shall destroy you!

MOMOTARO: Inu the Destroyer? Get lost, you flea-bitten mutt. I am on my way to slay the Oni, and I can slay you if I have to! I am Momotaro, sent by the gods.

NARRATOR: The dog fell down onto its haunches and yelped.

INU: *(yelping)* Momotaro? You're that freaky peach boy! Please! Don't kill me! I have so much to live for! So many things to sniff!

MOMOTARO: *(confused)* You have heard of me?

INU: *Everybody* knows Momotaro! You were born out of a peach. The rumor is that you will either save the world—or destroy it. Just please don't destroy *me*.

NARRATOR: A sly smile spread over the boy's face.

MOMOTARO: Who is "the Destroyer" now? *(loudly)* Yes, I am Momotaro, the mighty and terrible. Now, give me one good reason I don't end your miserable life right now.

INU: I can help you! It's a dog-eat-dog world out there. I can give you my protection.

MOMOTARO: Hmmmm. All right. I'll let you live. And, here!

INU: Dumplings!

NARRATOR: Momotaro threw the dog a dumpling, which he greedily gobbled up.

INU: *(smacking sounds)* You are most kind, Lord Momotaro! Oooh. Nice texture.

MOMOTARO: Come, Inu. I'm headed to the Island-Kingdom of the Oni.

INU: *(gulping)* Oh.

MOMOTARO: Having second thoughts?

INU: Of course not! Lead the way, master!

NARRATOR: The two new companions walked on until the road took them through a dark grove. At once, the hairs on the back of the dog's neck stood up.

INU: *(whispering)* Master, my canine senses are tingling! We are being watched from above. *(sniffing the air)*

MOMOTARO: What do you smell?

INU: Something dirty—and tricky—with opposable thumbs—it must be a…

NARRATOR: Inu would have finished his sentence, but a rock struck him on the nose.

INU: *(in pain)* Aroooo! My nose! My nose! Watch out, master! It's a deadly assassin!

MOMOTARO: Or just another member of the animal kingdom.

NARRATOR: The boy turned and addressed the nearest tree.

MOMOTARO: Whoever or whatever you are, come down so that we can see you.

NARRATOR: No movement came from the treetop.

MOMOTARO: *(grandly)* This is Momotaro speaking! Don't make me come up there!

NARRATOR: A furry face appeared among the leaves and let out a shrill cry. *(monkey chatter)*

SARU: Did you say Momotaro?

MOMOTARO: Yes.

INU: Grrr. I knew it! It's that pesky primate, Saru!

SARU: Call off that furry, four-legged fleabag, and I will address you, Lord Momotaro.

NARRATOR: A monkey dropped from the branches onto Momotaro's shoulder. *(thump)*

SARU: I am Saru the Monkey. You must be the peach-boy that everyone speaks of. I apologize that I did not recognize you. I would not expect you to be traveling with such riff-raff. Or should I say, riff-ruff?

INU: *(angrily)* Let me at him! Let me at him! I'll rip him apart!

MOMOTARO: I see you two have a history.

SARU: Yes, Inu "the Destroyer," and I go way back. I can't count the times that I've pelted him with rocks and sent him running away with his tail tucked between his legs.

INU: You cowardly furrball! If I could reach you, I would end your life!

SARU: Too bad you canines are so vertically challenged.

MOMOTARO: Be quiet, you two! Saru, apologize to Inu.

SARU: Fine. *(to Inu)* I'm soooo sorry for putting a widdle boo-boo on your precious, doggy-woggy snout.

INU: *(growling)* One wrong step, banana-breath, and I'll have your tail for a chew-toy!

SARU: Ah, shut your muzzle.

MOMOTARO: Saru, now that you have apologized—although not very sincerely—you may be on your way.

SARU: Well, the truth is I don't have anywhere to go. All I do is sit in that tree there all day and throw rocks at travelers. As fulfilling as rock-chucking is, I still feel… empty.

MOMOTARO: We are headed for the Island-Kingdom and the Oni fortress. Would you care to accompany us?

SARU: Ha! I had always heard that you would either save the world—or destroy it. Either way, I'd love to come with you—just to see the show.

INU: *(whispering)* No, no, master! We don't need a scoundrel like him around! He will betray us for sure. You can never trust a tree-dweller.

NARRATOR: Suddenly another rock bounced off Inu's nose.

INU: Argh! Stop that!

SARU: Would you prefer that I threw something else? Monkeys *are* famous for throwing worse things, you know.

MOMOTARO: Just stick to rocks. Saru, your skills might come in handy. You may accompany us. I will even give you a bit of my mother's dumplings for your trouble.

SARU: Ooooh. Dumplings! *(smacking sounds)*

NARRATOR: The peach-boy and his companions continued on—Saru perched on his shoulder and Inu walking behind him, rubbing an injured snout. Soon through the trunks of the trees, Momotaro could see the sea far in the distance.

MOMOTARO: The sea at last! Once we reach the shore we will have to commandeer a boat to get us over to the Island-Kingdom. I hope the boatman allows pets aboard.

INU: Maybe he'll have a strict No-Monkey policy.

SARU: *(dog-whistle)* Hey, Rover. Why don't you go fetch something?

MOMOTARO: You two, stop your bickering!

NARRATOR: Their conversation was interrupted by a sudden flurry of feathers, and a pheasant landed in the path before them. Robes of feathers hung from the pheasant's body, and on its head it wore a scarlet cap. As the three companions stared at the pheasant in awed silence, it bowed grandly before them.

MOMOTARO: What an amazing bird!

INU: Yes. *(yelling)* Kill it!

SARU: I get a drumstick!

MOMOTARO: No! Wait!

NARRATOR: Inu and Saru, not heeding their master, charged forward.

KIJI: *(sagely)* Hmmm.

NARRATOR: The pheasant flew into action—baring his razor-sharp spurs and slicing them through the air. *(sound of dazzling fighting move)*

KIJI: *(battlecry)* Aiieeeee!

INU AND SARU: Aiieeee! Retreat! Retreat!

NARRATOR: Momotaro chuckled as the pheasant flogged Inu and Saru into submission. (*flogging and whimpering noises*) The monkey and dog ran and hid behind their master.

INU: (*in fright*) G-g-get that b-b-bird away from me!

SARU: That's one foul fowl!

NARRATOR: The pheasant bowed nobly toward his opponents.

KIJI: A wise bird once said, "'Tis the gentle wing which strikes with the most strength." I am the one called Kiji the Sage. I have heard of your quest, Lord Momotaro, and would like to join you.

MOMOTARO: How did—?

KIJI: A little birdie told me, of course.

SARU: No deal. Listen, Momo, we definitely don't need the help of Mr. Fortune Cookie here.

MOMOTARO: Why not? He is a skilled fighter. He beat you and Inu easily enough.

SARU: Do you really want an annoying, talking animal tagging along?

MOMOTARO: Why not? I already have you two. What's one more? (*to Kiji*) Kiji, you are most welcome! Forgive my furry friends. Here is a dumpling for your trouble.

KIJI: Ah, I am ever in your debt!

MOMOTARO: Now listen, you all must learn to get along. The only way we can defeat the Oni is as a team!

SARU: Oh yes! Teamwork! (*whispering to Inu*) Okay, listen up, dog. We'll wait until the bird's distracted. Then we'll have those drumsticks after all.

NARRATOR: When they reached the seaside, they saw the smoking remains of a village. They found a frightened fisherman hiding within one of the blackened huts.

MOMOTARO: Did the Oni do this?

FISHERMAN: Yes, and they dragged all the others away across the sea. We are lost! Lost!

MOMOTARO: Do not worry. I am Momotaro, and I am going to the Island-Kingdom to defeat them.

FISHERMAN: No, please! You will only make them angry. If you challenge them, it will be the end of the world!

MOMOTARO: Then I will either save the world—or destroy it.

NARRATOR: The fisherman showed them a fishing boat that was still intact. Momotaro loaded the animals into the boat and, hoisting the sail, steered it toward the Island-Kingdom. A black storm-cloud of doom hung over the distant isle.

MOMOTARO: There it is.

SARU: Cheery place.

NARRATOR: As they sailed, the huge sea swells tossed their small boat roughly up and down.

INU: Grrr. I do not like being at sea.

SARU: At least you can dog-paddle.

KIJI: This is quite a bumpy ride. But as a wise bird once said, "It is the rough road that leads to true wisdom."

SARU: It is the wise bird that buttons his beak.

MOMOTARO: Enough bickering!

INU: Master is right. Separate we are nothing. We can only defeat our enemy… together.

KIJI: *(sickly)* I think I'm going to be sick!

INU: Well, *you* try coming up with an inspirational speech off the top of your head.

KIJI: *(gurgling)* No, I fear I am actually going to be sick. I am not fit for sea travel.

NARRATOR: Finally, the menacing cliffs of the Oni Island-Kingdom loomed up before them, casting a shadow over their small craft.

MOMOTARO: Remember, friends, we are nearing an island of devils, who will rip us limb from limb if we are not careful. They will drink our blood and snack on our sinews.

KIJI: *(gurgling)* Oh my. Such detail.

SARU: Is this supposed to be a pep talk?

MOMOTARO: We will need someone to go ahead of the rest of us and create a diversion.

SARU: I nominate the bird.

INU: Second.

MOMOTARO: Kiji, are you well enough to fly?

KIJI: I will do anything to get off this turbulent craft!

NARRATOR: The sickly pheasant took to the air, flying up to the heights of the cliffs, where the jagged towers of the Oni fortress stood. Horned archers stood guard upon the walls and observed Kiji's approach.

ONI: Bird! Shoot it down! Shoot it down!

NARRATOR: A hail of arrows flew through the air toward Kiji, who bobbed and weaved to avoid the deadly darts. *(shoom, shoom, shoom)*

KIJI: *(gurgling)* Ooooh. My poor stomach!

NARRATOR: The guards sounded an alarm, and the red bodies of a thousand evil Oni poured out of their crooked fortress like bees from a hive. They brandished their iron clubs, jumped up into the air, and shouted vile curses at the bird as he flew above.

KIJI: *(shouting)* Beware, you ornery Oni! Beware! Momotaro is coming! He's coming for your heads!

ONI: *(mocking voice)* Peach boy? Oh no! Not him! We are soooo frightened! What are you? His chicken assassin?

NARRATOR: All the Oni laughed and continued to hurl arrows, spears, and insults at Kiji until he landed on the tallest spire of the fortress. Kiji watched the Oni circling far below him chanting. *(all Oni chanting, "Kill the bird! Kill the bird!")*

KIJI: Oooh. (*gurgling*) I would stop that circling if I were you…uh-oh! (*puking sound*)

(*cries of disgust from all the Oni*)

ONI: Aaiieee! The bird is attacking us!

KIJI: Oh! That worked quite well! (*puking sound*) Take that! And that! Ha! I feel much better now.

NARRATOR: Hearing the commotion outside, the Oni King appeared on the steps of the fortress. His body and his horns dwarfed those of the other Oni. He snarled up at the pheasant.

ONI KING: By my horns, you fools are worthless! One of you imbeciles climb up there and kill that barfing bird, or I'll kill you myself!

NARRATOR: As the Oni rushed to obey his orders, Kiji realized his diversion was a success.

KIJI: Ha-ha! I may have lost my lunch, but I have gained my objective.

NARRATOR: Far below the mountaintop fortress Momotaro, Inu, and Saru were sneaking ashore. There was no visible way to scale up the sheer cliffs.

MOMOTARO: Look! There is a cave. Let us search for a passageway in there.

NARRATOR: Inside the cave, they found a flowing stream, and they followed it deeper into the rock. Suddenly two white forms appeared in the darkness ahead of them.

SARU: (*frightened*) Ghosts! I'm out of here!

INU: No, they smell human.

NARRATOR: It was two maidens, dressed all in white, weeping as they washed their laundry in the stream.

SARU: Oooh! Fine-looking ladies!

MOMOTARO: Greetings, maidens. Who are you and why do you weep?

NARRATOR: The maidens jumped when they heard the boy's voice.

MAIDEN ONE: Ah! Who are you?

MOMOTARO: I am Momotaro. I have come here to defeat the Oni.

MAIDEN ONE: We always heard of the peach boy who would either destroy the world—or save it.

MAIDEN TWO: You're a little short to be a mighty warrior, aren't you? And who are these strange animals?

SARU: You have caught *my* eye as well, sweetheart.

MAIDEN TWO: Ew.

MAIDEN ONE: Noble Momotaro, we are human maidens who were captured by Oni.

MAIDEN TWO: (*sniffling*) Those demons did horrible, ghastly things to us.

MOMOTARO: They tortured you?

MAIDEN TWO: Worse! They made us…do laundry! We are the daughters of rich lords. These hands should never touch dirty garments.

MOMOTARO: Is that why you weep?

MAIDEN ONE: Not only that, but also because our family was killed.

MAIDEN TWO: Oh yeah. That, too.

MAIDEN ONE: The humans who were captured with us have been devoured by the Oni one by one. That is why we are here washing these blood-soaked clothes.

MAIDEN TWO: Have you ever tried to get bloodstains out of clothing? It's horrible!

MOMOTARO: Then weep no more. I will rescue you.

MAIDEN TWO: You? How can some peachy warrior defeat fearsome Oni?

MOMOTARO: I am not alone. I have my animal companions to help.

NARRATOR: Inu and Saru swelled with pride.

MAIDEN TWO: Let's see…an undergrown weakling, a mutt, and a monkey against man-eating monsters. *(snotty laugh)* Good luck.

MAIDEN ONE: No, sister. This young man seems brave and true. He is worthy of our father's sword.

NARRATOR: The maiden pulled a finely crafted sword from their laundry basket.

SARU: And why do you bring a sword to do your laundry?

MAIDEN TWO: Hey, laundry can be dangerous business.

NARRATOR: So the laundry maidens presented Momotaro with their father's massive sword.

MOMOTARO: Thank you for this! I will not let you down!

NARRATOR: Saru hopped forward and held the second maiden's hand in his own.

SARU: Wait for me, my sweet.

MAIDEN TWO: Ew.

MOMOTARO: Come on! We must find Kiji and rescue the other prisoners here.

NARRATOR: They continued the path of the tunnel, and it led them ever upward. When it seemed that they must be close to the mountaintop at last, the tunnel was suddenly blocked by a pair of massive, metal doors, a giant lock hanging from them. The evil symbols of the Oni were inscribed there.

MOMOTARO: The maidens did not tell us about this.

SARU: The Oni must have tightened security since the laundry left!

MOMOTARO: Stand back.

NARRATOR: Momotaro raised his new sword and hacked at the doors with all his might, but the lock would not give. *(clang, clang, clang)*

INU: Wait a minute, Master. My teeth are sharper than any iron.

NARRATOR: Inu took the lock between his teeth and bore down. The lock shattered. *(shattering noise)*

MOMOTARO: Ha! I knew you would come in handy someday.

INU: We dogs are man's best friend for a reason!

NARRATOR: But even though the lock was shattered, Momotaro could not budge the doors.

MOMOTARO: There must be a release mechanism somewhere else. Examine the tunnel walls.

SARU: Leave this to me!

NARRATOR: Saru scaled up the doors into the darkness. There was a distant clicking sound, and the doors swung open.

SARU: Another point for the primates!

MOMOTARO: Quickly now! If Kiji has done his job right, we will have the element of surprise!

NARRATOR: Kiji had worked the Oni up into a fury. Time and time again they had tried scaling the tall spire that Kiji perched upon, only to fail. Now they were howling with rage and tearing at their beards. But a booming voice caused them to pause.

MOMOTARO: *(booming)* All right, you odious Oni. It's time that you picked on someone your own size!

ONI: Huh?

NARRATOR: The Oni turned. At the sight of Momotaro the Oni King only sneered.

ONI KING: *(laugh)* Look at this half-pint! Kill him at once! He is no threat to us!

NARRATOR: Saru and Inu stepped bravely forward. Kiji, too, swooped down and landed by his master.

INU: *(growling)* He does not fight alone.

ONI KING: We do not fear mangy dogs, cheeky monkeys, or vomiting birds. Oni warriors, attack! Kill them all!

NARRATOR: The Oni army attacked, and the battle was ferocious. *(sounds of battle)* Momotaro's sword cut this way and that. Inu bit at the Oni's ankles. Saru scooped up an armload of rocks and chucked them with deadly skill. Kiji swooped down and flogged at the Oni with his savage spurs. Soon the Oni were so beaten, bruised, and confused that they ran about wildly.

Saru stretched a rope near the cliff's edge—tripping a herd of fleeing Oni, who fell to their deaths. *(sounds of falling Oni)*

ONI KING: Enough of this foolishness!

NARRATOR: From amid the fray, the Oni King flew against Momotaro, bashing his iron club against the warrior's sword. *(clang, clang, clang)* Finally, Momotaro fell to the ground under the onslaught. The Oni King brought his massive, gnarled foot down upon Momotaro—pinning him to the ground.

ONI KING: Ha! You foolish peach-slice! You thought you could defeat me—a lord among demons?

NARRATOR: Inu, Saru, and Kiji stopped their own battles—staring in shock at their master being crushed by the Oni king.

ONI KING: No power on earth can defeat me! Now, I will juice you, peach-boy!

NARRATOR: Just then Momotaro's face began to glow with a strange, orange light.

MOMOTARO: You may be right. No power on earth can defeat you. But I am Momotaro—sent from heaven!

NARRATOR: With superhuman strength, Momotaro threw the Oni King from him.

ONI KING: *(cry of fright)* Aiiieee!

NARRATOR: Momotaro rose, taller and more powerful than before.

MOMOTARO: You will learn not to *pit* yourself against the power of the peach!

NARRATOR: The Oni King raised his iron club to defend himself, but Momotaro sliced it in half. *(shing)* The Oni King fell at Momotaro's feet, defeated.

ONI KING: *(sniveling)* Please! Spare me, powerful lord! Forgive me! Forgive me!

MOMOTARO: Forgive you? You and your Oni have devoured innocent humans. How do you justify such a horrible crime?

ONI KING: We were hungry! And humans are so tasty. They are a part of our food chain, you know.

NARRATOR: Momotaro turned to his animal companions.

MOMOTARO: What should I do, friends? Should I spare them?

INU: Well, you have definitely made a monkey out of him.

SARU: Yes, and you already made him beg like a dog. Very shameful.

KIJI: It is only a true beast that will not spare a conquered foe.

MOMOTARO: Very well, my wise friends. *(to the Oni King)* Monster, I will spare you if you agree to three things. First, free all of your captives. Secondly, return all the treasure you have stolen. Thirdly, cut off your horns and, therefore, become kindly spirits. Then do good to the world as you have always done evil.

ONI KING: Done! Done! And done! Thank you, Peach Boy, for sparing me.

NARRATOR: So Momotaro and his animal companions overthrew the Oni stronghold. The Oni's captives were freed and returned to their families. All of the stolen treasure that the Oni had amassed was returned to its rightful owners. Everyone in the countryside praised the heroism of Momotaro.

FISHERMAN: See? I always told you that boy would save the world!

NARRATOR: Much of the Oni treasure went unclaimed, as its original owners had died long ago, so Momotaro claimed this for himself.

SARU: *(sadly)* Well, what now? I guess it's back to the old life—chucking rocks… monkeying around.

INU: *(sadly)* Biting at fleas, barking up the wrong tree.

KIJI: *(sadly)* Sitting around in an empty nest.

MOMOTARO: No, my friends. That will not do! You will return home with me!

(cheers from all the animals)

NARRATOR: Kiji flapped his wings with excitement, and Inu and Saru embraced and then, realizing what they had done, quickly separated.

So Momotaro returned home to his elderly parents, and from that time on, they no longer lived in a simple hut. Instead, they lived in a great palace with their three animal companions, and everything was simply peachy.

DISCUSSION QUESTIONS

1. What are some reasons that Momotaro should be considered a hero?
2. How is Momotaro's adventure an example of a typical Hero's Journey?
3. Could Momotaro have succeeded without the help of his animal companions? Explain.
4. What lesson do Momotaro's animal companions learn about teamwork?
5. *Oni* is a Japanese word that can be translated as *ogre* or *demon*. Look at the illustration of the Oni on the first page. Is this how you pictured these creatures? Explain.
6. Heroes often have special circumstances in their early lives that show they are destined for greatness. How does the childhood of Momotaro foreshadow his future heroism?

ANANSI & THE SKY GOD'S STORIES TEACHER GUIDE

BACKGROUND

Anansi is the ultimate trickster. In some stories he appears as a regular spider, and in others he is a humanoid creature with spider-like powers. Although his physical description changes from time to time, some things never change: his crafty cunning and penchant for trouble. Originating in the stories of the Ashanti people of Ghana, the accomplishments of Anansi are many: the creation of the sun and moon, the stars and planets, agriculture and hunting. The list goes on and on. In fact, the character was so ubiquitous, all stories in Ghana are called "spider tales" in his honor. For all his kindly deeds, there is a dark side to Anansi, too. His tricks sometimes turn deadly—like when his trick of tying Tiger to a tree ends with Tiger's death at the hands of a hunter.

When the African Slave Trade ripped Africans from their homes and carried them to the New World, spider tales came with them—becoming popular among slaves in the Caribbean. Anansi's name transformed into "Aunt Nancy," but his tricks remained the same. Anansi, who was able to outwit those more powerful than he, served as a symbol of hope for slaves at the mercy of cruel slavemasters. Spider tales lived on.

SUMMARY

Anansi the spider watches the humans of earth and notices that they have nothing in life to bring them happiness. Then he remembers that the Sky God has special things called stories that allow those who hear them to forget their troubles for just a little while. Anansi resolves to ask Nyame the Sky God to share his stories. Anansi spins a web up into the sky and makes this request of the Sky God, who refuses unless Anansi completes a special mission for him. Anansi must capture four of the deadliest creatures on the earth: Mmoboro, a deadly hornet swarm, Osebo, a killer leopard, Onini, a strangling serpent, and Mmoatia, a tricky fairy. Anansi agrees, but before beginning his mission, he makes a plan for trapping the dangerous creatures with his wife, Aso, who is as clever as he is.

Anansi heads first to Mmboro the hornet swarm. Pouring a gourd full of water down over himself, Anansi convinces the hornets that it is raining and invites them to take shelter in the empty gourd. When they do, he seals them up inside.

Next Anansi digs a pit in the forest, where Osebo the leopard stalks, and traps the leopard within it. Anansi offers to help Osebo out of the pit, but he actually attaches him to a tree and slingshots him all the way up to the Sky God.

Anansi goes after Onini the python next and uses his excessive pride against him. Anansi tells Onini a false rumor about a snake longer than him and offers to measure the snake to prove that he is really the longest. To do so, Anansi offers to tie Onini to a fallen tree, and once he does so, transports the bound python to the Sky God.

Finally, Anansi faces off against Mmoatia the tricky fairy. To defeat her, he creates a human-like doll, covers it in sap, and gives it a tasty dish made from yams. The fairy appears and asks for some of the yams, and when the doll does not reply, the fairy attacks it and becomes entangled in the sap. Anansi takes her to the Sky God.

The Sky God is impressed that Anansi completed his challenge. He gives Anansi his stories, declaring that they will thenceforward be named "spider stories" in honor of Anansi.

ESSENTIAL QUESTIONS

- Why are stories so important?

ANTICIPATORY QUESTIONS

- What is a trickster?
- Why do human beings enjoy stories so much?

NAME PRONUNCIATIONS

Anansi	UH-NAHN-SĒ
Nyame	NIH-YAH-MĀ
Aso	Ā-SŌ
Mmboro	EM-BŌ-RŌ
Osebo	Ō-SĒ-BŌ
Onini	Ō-NĒ-NĒ
Mmoatia	MŌ-UH-TĒ-UH

CREATURE FEATURE

Anansi Anansi's appearance is a bit of an enigma. In some stories he is a normal-sized spider, who has the power to speak and reason. In others (like this one), he seems to be a combination of a spider and a man. In both instances, there are not many specific details about his appearance, so readers are left to wonder what the "spider-man" truly looks like.

TEACHABLE TERMS

- **Motif: Anthropomorphic Animals** Myth and folklore is full of anthropomorphic creatures (or animals with human-like qualities). The character Anansi blurs the line between human and animal so much that in some stories it is difficult to tell which he is.
- **Characterization** Discuss whether Anansi is selfless or selfish. On one hand, he wants to win stories for humans to make their lives better, but on the other hand, it seems he wants to win glory for himself.
- **Puns** As Anansi outwits the various creatures, he makes a variety of puns. On pg. 67 he tells the hornets "to put a cork in it" after he has corked them up inside the gourd. On pg. 68 he calls the tree that flung the leopard into the sky a "catapult." On pg. 69 he tells the python "don't be a strangler" instead of "stranger." On pg. 71 he tells the fairy she "looks like a sap" after getting trapped by sap. On pg. 71 he also declares, "I yam what I yam," a pun on the yams used in the fairy trap.
- **Symbol** This story presents stories as a symbol of hope. Anansi believes that if humans have stories, they will also have hope in life. Discuss the various ways that stories give people hope.

RECALL QUESTIONS

1. Who helps Anansi lay out his plans to achieve his quest?
2. How does Anansi deceive Mmboro the hornet swarm?
3. How does Anansi trick Onini the python?
4. How does Anansi trick Mmoatia the fairy?
5. What other creature does Anansi trap?

ANANSI
AND THE SKY GOD'S STORIES

CAST

ANANSI	*Spider-like Creature*
ASO	*Wife of Anansi*
SKY GOD	*Ruler of the Sky*
HORNET ONE	*Angry Insect*
HORNET TWO	*Angry Insect*
HORNET THREE	*Angry Insect*
OSEBO	*Deadly Leopard*
ONINI	*Strangling Python*
MMOATIA	*Tricky Fairy*

NARRATOR: It all started when Anansi was relaxing on his web one day. He had spun himself a web-hammock between two particularly tall trees, and he was lazily watching the humans of earth as they went to and fro.

Anansi and the Sky God's Stories 63

ANANSI: Poor creatures. They live such sad, empty lives. They work all day without anything to bring a smile to their faces. Then they go home at night, curl up in their beds, and wait for the morning to come—just so they can do it all again. It's downright depressing!

NARRATOR: Anansi was not a human. He looked human, but instead of two arms and two legs, he had eight limbs—like a spider—and he could spin webs. Although he was not quite human himself, Anansi loved humans and wanted to help them as much as he could.

ANANSI: Wait! That's it! I know how to improve the lives of these humans!

NARRATOR: Anansi skittered home as fast as his legs could carry him. Waiting in the doorway of his hut was Aso, his wife, who was just as clever as he.

ANANSI: Aso, I've figured it out! I can make the lives of humans so much better. And by better, I mean not so dull and boring!

ASO: *My* life is never dull and boring. I have *you* bringing all kinds of trouble into it.

ANANSI: You know how I can use my webs to go between this world and the palace of Nyame the Sky God above?

ASO: Uh-huh. It makes me dizzy just thinking about it.

ANANSI: Anyway, the last time I was there, the place was simply overflowing with stories.

ASO: *(in confusion)* What are stories?

ANANSI: Oh, they are the greatest things! Whenever you hear one of them, you forget all about your troubles. And the Sky God owns all the stories ever told—enough to tell for a thousand years! If humans had these stories, their lives would be so much better!

ASO: But you said all the stories belong to the Sky God.

ANANSI: Yes, but he has so many! Mounds and mounds of stories! So it wouldn't hurt him to share some of them with humans.

ASO: Oh, Anansi, your heart is good, but your head is soft. Don't you know that the Sky God does not like to share? He would never give up his stories—especially not for a bunch of earth-dwellers like us!

ANANSI: Oh, he would if *I* asked him to! I'm his favorite!

ASO: Dear, you are not as charming as you think you are.

ANANSI: Fine! Just watch! I'll go to the Sky God right now. I bet I come back with armloads of stories!

ASO: *(unconvinced)* Hmmm. Sounds good, dear. Be home in time for supper.

ANANSI: *(grumbling)* I'll show her.

NARRATOR: Storming out from his hut, Anansi began to fling his webbing high into the sky. *(Thwip! Thwip! Thwip!)* Anansi spun a ladder that reached all the way into the heavens. Any human would have become dizzy and fallen, but not Anansi.

Soon he reached the threshold of the Sky God's palace—a vast hall made from billowy clouds. Anansi strode boldly into its airy halls and found the Sky God seated upon his shimmering throne. All around the palace heaps and heaps of stories were piled upon one another.

ANANSI: Ahem! Your majesty, it is I—your favorite earth-dweller—Anansi!

NARRATOR: The Sky God stared down at Anansi unimpressed.

SKY GOD: *(sigh)* Well, if it isn't the amazing spider-man? What are you doing here, Anansi?

ANANSI: Oh, mighty Sky God! I just came to shoot the breeze. Heh heh. Get it? Shoot the breeze? With a Sky God?

SKY GOD: *(not amused)* Uh-huh. I know you're here because you want something. What is it?

ANANSI: Well, since you asked, I was hoping to request a teeny, tiny favor. I would like to…*(quickly)* borrow some of your stories to give to the humans.

SKY GOD: *(in shock)* What? You can't be serious! Stories are precious things! Why would I waste them on *humans*?

ANANSI: Well, for starters, they practically worship you! Don't you owe them something? They have sad, little lives that are filled with toil. Can't you spare them a bit of wonder?

NARRATOR: The Sky God stared at Anansi—his brow furrowed.

SKY GOD: Listen to me, spider—I will give up *none* of my stories.

ANANSI: Oh, okay then. *(softly)* I guess my wife was right.

SKY GOD: Your wife? What does she have to do with this?

ANANSI: She said you were the stingiest, most selfish, most thoroughly-uncaring Sky God she's ever seen.

SKY GOD: *(raging)* What?

NARRATOR: The Sky God's eyes crackled with lightning, and the palace's cloud-walls grew stormy and black. *(storm sounds)*

ANANSI: Uh…your majesty. Remember your atmospheric pressure! Maybe you're overreacting?

SKY GOD: *(roaring)* How dare you! I should squash you like an insect!

ANANSI: Technically, I'm an arachnid. And *I* didn't say these things about you. My wife did! But, you know, you could really make her eat her words by giving me some of your stories! Prove how kind you truly are.

NARRATOR: With a whoosh, the Sky God's rage blew over.

SKY GOD: Oh, I see what your game is. You're using one of your spider tricks on me. Well, it won't work!

ANANSI: You're onto me, huh?

SKY GOD: Oh yes. I've heard plenty of stories about your tricks. In fact, here's one right here, and the ink is still fresh!

NARRATOR: The Sky God picked up a scroll from the heap nearest to his throne.

SKY GOD: Hmmm. Let's see. It's called "Anansi Tricks the Mighty Tiger."

ANANSI: Oh, good one! Tricking that two-ton tabby cat was easy. I can trick any creature on earth!

SKY GOD: Oh really? Well, I will make you a deal then. If you bring me four creatures of my choosing, I will give *all of my* stories to mankind.

ANANSI: Really? Amazing!

SKY GOD: But I wonder what your motive is. I've never known you to think of anyone but yourself. Why do you want to help the humans so much?

ANANSI: Can't a spider-guy care about his fellow man?

SKY GOD: Anansi…

ANANSI: All right. All right. It's because I know that if I pull this off, it will be the greatest story ever told!

SKY GOD: *If* you don't come back dead. The creatures I'm sending you after are ferocious killers. First, there is Mmboro the Hornet swarm, whose stings cause fiery death.

ANANSI: Oooh. I've heard of them.

SKY GOD: Osebo the Leopard, whose teeth are like knives.

ANANSI: Sounds deadly.

SKY GOD: Onini the Python, whose coils can crush the life out of any creature.

ANANSI: Not fun.

SKY GOD: And Mmoatia the Fairy, whose mischievous magic can melt your mind.

ANANSI: Oh, my poor exoskeleton! Any one of those could kill me!

SKY GOD: Scared? Then give up and crawl back down your web in defeat.

ANANSI: Never! I accept this challenge! I will win stories for mankind, and humans will tell stories about me for the rest of time.

SKY GOD: Or the *defeat* of Anansi will become the greatest story ever told.

NARRATOR: Anansi put his eight limbs into motion and spun a line back down to earth.

ANANSI: That arrogant Sky God! Who does he think he is, anyway? To survive, I'll need help from the wisest person I know—apart from myself, that is.

NARRATOR: Anansi swung back to his hut where his wife had just finished the day's baking.

ASO: *(sarcastically)* What? Back so soon? And no stories? I'm shocked.

ANANSI: Listen, Aso. The Sky God gave me a chance! I just have to capture four of earth's deadliest creatures and then I can have his stories. What do you think about that?

ASO: I think I may soon be a widow.

ANANSI: Funny. Help me think. You know I love to try the impossible. Everyone said I couldn't win you as a wife, but I did.

ASO: One of your finer tricks. *(pause)* Fine. I will help you. But if you end up getting squashed, don't blame me.

NARRATOR: So Anansi told her about the four creatures he would need to trap, and Aso helped her husband lay out a plan.

ANANSI: Perfect! I never would have thought of that!

ASO: I know!

NARRATOR: Anansi set out, but not without first kissing his wife goodbye. He headed out in search of Mmboro the hornet swarm, whose sting was like fire. Everyone knew where they lived, but no one was foolish enough to approach their hive.

When the hornets heard Anansi approaching, they flew out of their nest at once. *(buzzing of a hornet swarm)*

HORNET ONE: *(buzzing)* Forward, men! Sting first! Ask questions later!

HORNET TWO: Aye, aye, sir!

HORNET THREE: Target dead ahead, sir!

NARRATOR: But to the swarm's shock, Anansi did not cower back in fear at their approach. He greeted them nonchalantly—holding a broad leaf over his head.

ANANSI: Oh, hello there, brother hornets! Can you believe this rain?

NARRATOR: The hornet swarm drew up at once.

HORNET ONE: Rain?

HORNET TWO: What rain?

HORNET THREE: We hate rain!

NARRATOR: In another hand Anansi held a calabash gourd filled with water, and he began to pour the water over the leaf. *(tinkling of water)*

ANANSI: Rain! See! You all better get inside soon!

HORNET ONE: It *is* rain!

HORNET TWO: Anger…building…

HORNET THREE: Argh! Rain makes us as mad as…well…a hornet!

NARRATOR: Anansi whirled the now-empty gourd into their view.

ANANSI: Why don't you all fly in here? It will keep you safe!

HORNET ONE: Sounds good to me!

HORNET TWO: Grand idea!

HORNET THREE: Thank you, non-suspicious stranger!

NARRATOR: So the deadly swarm of hornets crowded into the opening of the hollow gourd, which Anansi promptly plugged. He shook the gourd and giggled to himself.

HORNET ONE: Wait! Did he just trick us?

HORNET TWO: I think he did! Curse our tiny insect brains!

HORNET THREE: We'll get you for this, Anansi!

ANANSI: Ah, put a cork in it. Oh wait! I already did! *(giggle)* You stupid hornets! Give the Sky God my compliments.

NARRATOR: He hooked the gourd onto the end of one of his webs and slung it around his head until it was whizzing. *(whizzing sound)* Then he let it go—sending it up, up to the heavens. There was a faraway pop as it entered the clouds, which thundered a reply. *(thunder noises)*

SKY GOD: *(thundering)* One task down and three ahead. Watch out, Anansi, or you'll end up dead.

ANANSI: One down! Three to go!

NARRATOR: From there Anansi headed into the forest, the hunting grounds of Osebo, the leopard with teeth like knives.

ANANSI: Teeth like knives, huh? I'd prefer teeth like spoons! Osebo is so stealthy, he can walk through the grass without even rustling it, but he's also not very observant. I hope Aso's plan works, or I'll be cat food.

NARRATOR: Anansi dug a pit in the middle of the forest in a spot he knew Osebo was sure to pass. Then he covered up the hole with leaves and sticks. Anansi plopped his abdomen down on the far side of the pit and began to moan loudly.

ANANSI: *(bad acting)* Oh my! Lost in the forest again. Poor, little me! So fat and juicy!

NARRATOR: His cries ricocheted through the trees, reaching Osebo, who began licking his jaws and grinding his teeth against one another at the thought of prey.

OSEBO: Oh boy, oh boy, oh boy! A fat and juicy kill!

NARRATOR: The leopard did stalk stealthily—not even rustling the grass—and he spotted Anansi sitting alone in the forest. But he did not notice Anansi's trap, and as he prepared to spring, he fell down into the pit. *(crashing sound)*

OSEBO: Argh! Help! Help! I've fallen and I can't get out!

NARRATOR: Anansi came to the edge of the pit looking concerned.

ANANSI: Why, Osebo! You've fallen into a pit! How clumsy of you! Have you been hitting the cat nip again?

OSEBO: Anansi! I should have known it was you! You eight-legged freak!

ANANSI: How are those teeth of yours—still sharp as knives?

OSEBO: *(snarling)* Let me out of here, and I'll show you!

ANANSI: What a great idea! I'm sure you wouldn't immediately murder me and my entire family, would you?

OSEBO: Uh…of course not!

ANANSI: All right! Good to hear!

(Thwip! Thwip!)

NARRATOR: Anansi hooked his webbing onto a tall tree and bent it down to the opening of the pit. *(bending sound)*

ANANSI: Here you are, dear friend. I'll just use my webs to hook you onto this tree, and when I cut it loose, it will lift you out.

OSEBO: Perfect! Then I can *thank* you with my very own mouth.

ANANSI: Oh, how kind!

(Thwip! Thwip! Thwip!)

NARRATOR: Once Anansi had the cat cocooned, he latched him onto the bent-over tree.

ANANSI: Give the Sky God my regards!

OSEBO: Sky God? Why would I—?

NARRATOR: Anansi used his spider leg to slice loose the bent tree. *(Sproing!)*

OSEBO: *(distant screaming)* Ahhhhhhh!

NARRATOR: It shot the leopard high, high into the sky, where he at last disappeared into the clouds.

ANANSI: That was quite a cat-apult.

NARRATOR: The heavens thundered down at Anansi. *(sounds of thunder)*

SKY GOD: Of my creatures you have captured two, but the ones that follow may capture *you*.

ANANSI: *(laughing)* Two down, two to go.

NARRATOR: Next Anansi headed deeper into the underbrush. Onini the giant python could choke the life out of any victim, but he was also horribly vain. Aso had given Anansi the perfect plan for trapping him.

Anansi was walking through the trees, running the plan over in his mind, when Onini fell out of nowhere onto his shoulders.

ONINI: Ssssurprise, sssspider.

NARRATOR: The python tightened its powerful coils around Anansi's neck.

ANANSI: *(choking)* Onini, old friend. I'm glad to see you. I was hoping you might settle a bet my wife and I were having.

ONINI: Let'sss hug firsssst. Then we can converssssse later.

ANANSI: Fair enough. *(gasp)* We wanted to tell you about another snake we met—one that was… much… bigger… than… you…

NARRATOR: Onini's coils loosened.

ONINI: What did you sssay? Ssspeak!

ANANSI: *(gasping for breath)* Quite a grip you have there, friend.

ONINI: Tell me about thisss other sssnake or you'll feel my grip again!

ANANSI: Oh, I'm not convinced he's longer than you—although my wife is *just positive* he's the longest snake in the world.

ONINI: How big isss he? Tell me! Tell me now, ssspider man!

ANANSI: Oh, he's about as long as this fallen tree lying here.

ONINI: Thisss one! Ha! I'm longer than that easssy!

ANANSI: Are you? You're so coil-y. It's hard to tell.

ONINI: Look! Look!

NARRATOR: Onini twisted around the fallen tree, but he could not make himself completely straight.

ANANSI: You're definitely close. Let's see. You keep coiling up at the ends. Why don't I tie you to it? That way we can know for sure.

ONINI: Ingeniousss!

NARRATOR: So the mighty python allowed Anansi to tie him to the tree.

ANANSI: I made sure those ropes are good and tight. Try curling now.

ONINI: I can't at all! Now sssay it! I'm the biggessst!

ANANSI: You are—and also the dumbessst!

ONINI: What?

ANANSI: Thank you, my friend, for allowing me to tie you. Now it will be no problem transporting you to the Sky God's palace. So handy! Snake-on-a-stick!

ONINI: Ansssssi, you no-good cheat!

NARRATOR: Anansi called out to a passing flock of birds and asked them to carry Onini up to the Sky God. He hooked them onto the fallen tree, and Onini was lifted into the sky.

ANANSI: Farewell, Onini. And don't be a strangler—I mean, stranger.

ONINI: *(yelling)* Anansssi! Anansssi!

NARRATOR: The heavens thundered down their receipt of the third offering. *(booming thunder)*

SKY GOD: Three earthly creatures you have caught, but trap the fourth one you will not.

ANANSI: *(laughing)* Three down, one to go.

NARRATOR: For his final challenge, Anansi would have to trap the mischievous fairy Mmoatia, whose tricks were just as mighty as his. She could turn herself invisible, and her pranks were often lethal.

ANANSI: I will meet this fairy, but first some arts and crafts.

NARRATOR: Anansi put his many arms to work cutting down a tree. Then from the wood he whittled a life-sized doll in the shape of a little girl—complete with dancing eyes and a mocking smirk.

ANANSI: Perfect.

NARRATOR: He covered the doll all over with the sticky sap from the tree and then carefully carried it into the hills, where Mmoatia lived. No one dared to go there because they feared the fairy's pranks.

ANANSI: I'll have to be careful, or I'll get stuck myself.

NARRATOR: He sat the doll down beneath a tree—as if she were having a picnic.

ANANSI: Now for a little ano.

NARRATOR: Following his wife's recipe, Anansi made some ano, a tasty dish made from yams.

ANANSI: And Aso said I couldn't cook! I call this dish "yam surprise."

NARRATOR: Then into the doll's cupped hands he placed the dish, which was so fragrant it could be smelled for miles.

ANANSI: All right! The trap is set.

NARRATOR: Anansi hid behind a nearby rock and flicked his legs together—counting off the seconds. *(magical sound)* Suddenly there was a shimmering in the air right before the doll. Colors flashed in all directions—a blinding kaleidoscope of light—and the tricky fairy stepped into the visible world.

MMOATIA: Foolish mortal! How dare you enter the realm of—oooh! Are those yams?

NARRATOR: The fairy crouched down and sniffed at the dish, but the doll just stared back at her blankly.

MMOATIA: *(angrily)* I said, "Are those yams?" Speak, mortal!

NARRATOR: The doll did not respond.

MMOATIA: Oh, you are rude! Don't you know who I am? I am Mmoatia the fairy! And these are my hills, see? Fear me, and obey!

NARRATOR: The doll did not seem to know who the fairy was.

MMOATIA: That's it!

NARRATOR: The fairy smacked the doll directly on her rosy cheek. *(Slap!)* To her shock, she found her hand stuck fast.

MMOATIA: *(grunting)* Let go! Let go, you little beast!

NARRATOR: The fairy struck at the doll with her other hand. *(Slap!)* And it stuck fast as well. Then she lashed out with her foot. *(Kick!)*

MMOATIA: Argh! What…is…happening?

NARRATOR: Soon her entire body had become entangled in the sap, and the fairy collapsed into a sticky, helpless heap.

ANANSI: Well, well, well. Someone sure looks like a sap!

NARRATOR: Anansi strolled up on the struggling fairy.

MMOATIA: Anansi! I should have known!

ANANSI: Stealing yams from a child? Tsk. Tsk.

MMOATIA: You, low-down, no-good, lying trickster!

ANANSI: I yam what I yam. Now if you don't mind, we have a meeting with the Sky God. I want to deliver you to him in person!

MMOATIA: Not the webbing!

(Thwip! Thwip! Thwip!)

MMOATIA: Ugh. Disgusting.

NARRATOR: Aso was waiting for Anansi when he arrived home with the webbed-up fairy.

ASO: You have been busy, husband. I heard the Sky God thundering his displeasure. I trust you've been successful with all *my* plans.

ANANSI: *Our* plans, yes. Now all I have to do is go to the Sky God and claim my prize.

ASO: Don't blow it.

NARRATOR: Aso planted a kiss on her husband's cheek, and Anansi spun another ladder up into the sky. There he entered the Sky God's palace—his four captives piled before the god's throne. *(groaning from the captured creatures)*

SKY GOD: Impressive. I thought for sure you would fail. Otherwise, I would never have wagered my stories.

ANANSI: You underestimated me. It's been done before, but it's dangerous. Just ask these sad-sacks.

SKY GOD: It is odd that the four most powerful creatures in the world could be beaten by one of the weakest.

ANANSI: I have a secret weapon.

SKY GOD: Your wife?

ANANSI: My wits.

NARRATOR: Anansi could tell the Sky God was trying to hide a smile.

ANANSI: Tell me, your majesty, are you unhappy that I have won?

SKY GOD: I am sad to lose my stories, but I see that you are a worthy keeper for them. Go, Anansi! Take my stories to earth. But from now on, they will be called "spider stories" in your honor.

NARRATOR: Anansi bowed low to the ground.

ANANSI: Thank you, my lord. I can think of no greater gift than that.

NARRATOR: It all came true—just as the Sky God had said. To this day it is hard to experience the joy of a story without thinking of Anansi and the great gift he gave all of us who dwell on earth.

DISCUSSION QUESTIONS

1. How is Anansi a good example of a trickster-hero?
2. Is Aso as much of a hero as Anansi is?
3. Is Anansi right—do stories make life better for humans? Explain.
4. Do you feel sorry for the captured creatures?
5. Are Anansi's motives selfless or selfish? Explain.
6. Does Anansi deserve to have stories renamed "spider stories" in his honor? Explain.

VASILISA THE BRAVE
TEACHER GUIDE

BACKGROUND

Russian folklore is full of frightening creatures lurking in the forest—the plant-like Leshi who waylays travelers and the beautiful Rusalka who lures young men to a watery death. But no forest-dwelling monster is as deadly as Baba Yaga, the ogress witch who loves to feast on human flesh. Her cottage stands upon two chicken legs and spins around when unwanted guests try to approach the doorway. Her yard is surrounded by a fence made from human bones and a talking gate that alerts her when guests attempt to escape. When traveling, Baba Yaga flies through the air in a huge mortar and uses her pestle to steer. With a broom, she sweeps away all evidence of her passing. All who know her, fear her.

Yet Baba Yaga is more than just a forest-dwelling witch. She is an ancient being with arcane powers—the protector of waters of immortality. Heroes have gone to her for assistance, and she has rewarded them with magical objects in return for their bravery and wit.

SUMMARY

Vasilisa lives in the woods with her father and mother, but her mother becomes ill and dies. Before she passes away, Vasilisa's mother gives her a doll and blesses it so it will comfort her. After Vasilisa's mother dies, her father remarries to a cruel woman, who brings along two nasty stepsisters. The three of them are mean to Vasilisa when her father is away. The stepmother comes up with a plan to get rid of Vasilisa for good. After dousing all the fires in the house, she tells Vasilisa she must go and fetch fire from an old woman who lives deep in the forest.

As Vasilisa prepares to face this task, her doll speaks to her—telling her that her stepmother is sending her to the home of Baba Yaga the witch, which means certain death. The doll tells Vasilisa to take four things along with her into the forest: cornmeal, bacon, rolls, and oil. Vasilisa does so. As Vasilisa travels through the forest, two mysterious riders pass her (one red and one black), and as they pass the time of day changes.

When Vasilisa reaches Baba Yaga's cottage, she sees that it is alive and standing on two chicken legs. The doll tells her to spread the cornmeal on the ground, and as the cottage bends over to eat it, Vasilisa jumps inside its doorway. Inside she comes face to face with Baba Yaga herself, who declares she has Vasilisa trapped and will eat her unless she completes an impossible task for her: laundering an enormous pile of Baba Yaga's clothes by midnight. Then Baba Yaga flies away in her mortar and pestle, vowing to return at midnight and eat Vasilisa.

The doll tells Vasilisa to give the bacon to Baba Yaga's cat, who is her servant. The cat is so grateful that it tells Vasilisa how to take some of Baba Yaga's fire from her home and gives her a magic comb to use if Baba Yaga chases her. As Vasilisa is leaving, Baba Yaga's dogs try to stop her, but the doll tells Vasilisa to feed them the rolls. The fence gate tries to cry out as Vasilisa goes through it, but the doll tells her to use the oil on its hinges to keep it quiet. Vasilisa takes a skull containing blue fire from Baba Yaga's fence. As Vasilisa is escaping through the woods, Baba Yaga returns home, finds the girl missing and flies after her. Vasilisa throws down the magic comb, which becomes a forest of tall trees and blocks Baba Yaga's pathway. Vasilisa arrives home, and the doll tells Vasilisa to show the skull to her stepmother and her stepsisters. The skull comes to life and chases them into the forest. Vasilisa is now free of her stepmother and stepsisters—thanks to her magic doll.

ESSENTIAL QUESTION

- Why is it important to be brave in the face of fear?

ANTICIPATORY QUESTIONS

- What are some details you know about witches? Where do they live? What do they look like? How do they travel?
- What is a mortar and pestle?
- Has a family member ever given you a special item that has sentimental value?

CONNECT

Other Vasilisa Folktales The story of Vasilisa has many different versions. In another version of the tale, Vasilisa does not have a magic doll, and when she braves the terrors of Baba Yaga's home, she instead relies on advice given to her by her aunt. Another version adds an especially happy ending onto the story. After ridding herself of her wicked stepmother, Vasilisa goes to live in Russia's capital city, where she works for a seamstress. Vasilisa's weaving is so wonderful that her work attracts the attention of the Tsarevich, the son of the Tsar or King. When the Tsarevich meets Vasilisa, he falls in love immediately and marries her. In yet another version of the story, far removed from this one, Vasilisa is a princess who has been turned into a frog.

NAME PRONUNCIATIONS

| Baba Yaga | BAH-BAH YAH-GUH |
| Vasilisa | VAH-SUH-LIH-SUH |

TEACHABLE TERMS

- **Motif** Stepmothers and stepsisters are a common motif in folktales. In previous centuries death by childbirth was common, and many fathers remarried merely to keep their household functioning. Many children had step-mothers and stepsiblings.
- **Simile** On pg. 76 the narrator says Vasilisa's new stepmother has a heart as cold as an empty fireplace.
- **Personification: The Red, Black, and White Riders** The three riders that Vasilisa encounters are personifications of the times of day. The red rider brings the sunset, the black rider brings nightfall, and the white rider brings the dawn.

RECALL QUESTIONS

1. Why does Vasilisa's stepmother send her into the forest?
2. What special gift did Vasilisa's mother give to her before she died?
3. What item does Baba Yaga's cat give to Vasilisa?
4. How does Baba Yaga travel?
5. How does Vasilisa defeat her stepmother and stepsisters?

VASILISA THE BRAVE

CAST

VASILISA	Brave young girl
MOTHER	Vasilisa's mother
DOLL	Gift to Vasilisa
STEPMOTHER	Cruel woman
STEPSISTER ONE	Cruel girl
STEPSISTER TWO	Cruel girl
BABA YAGA	Hideous, old witch
CAT	Servant to Baba Yaga
DOG	Servant to Baba Yaga
GATE	Servant to Baba Yaga

NARRATOR: There once was a little girl named Vasilisa, who was poor, yet somehow had everything she needed to be happy. She lived in a meager hut in the midst of the vast forest with her loving father and mother.

Her father was seldom home, working long hours afar, and her mother took good care of Vasilisa in his absence. But one day her mother became very ill and took to her bed. It seemed that she would soon die, so she called Vasilisa to her.

MOTHER: *(weakly)* My little girl! How I wish I could have watched you grow into a woman! But I feel my time to depart this world is near.

VASILISA: *(crying)* Oh, Mother! Don't leave me! I will be so afraid without you.

MOTHER: No. My little Vasilisa, you will be brave.

VASILISA: Aren't *you* afraid?

MOTHER: Vasilisa, remember this—if you start down the path of fear, you will never know where to stop.

NARRATOR: Then Vasilisa's mother pulled a little rag doll from beneath the blankets. Its eyes were carefully stitched to be lifelike and vibrant—just the same color as Vasilisa's mother's. Two long braids escaped from beneath its little head scarf.

MOTHER: I made this for you, and I have blessed it. Whenever you feel afraid, hold it close and know that I am with you.

NARRATOR: Vasilisa cried and cried, but her mother still passed from the world. Then all that she had left of her mother was the little doll.

VASILISA: Mother told me not to fear, so I will not be afraid—no matter what happens!

NARRATOR: It was good that Vasilisa resolved not to fear because her life became bleaker still. Her father, who worked himself to exhaustion, could not take care of the household, so he soon married again. This new stepmother, a bony, harsh woman, had a heart as cold as an empty fireplace.

STEPMOTHER: Listen to me, Vasilisa! If you're going to live under *my* roof, you'll have to earn your keep. There'll be no handouts here! Now go chop some wood for the fire!

NARRATOR: She brought two stepdaughters along with her to live in the forest hut.

STEPSISTER ONE: Look at that ugly doll!

STEPSISTER TWO: That's a doll? Ha! I thought it was an old rag! *(to Vasilisa)* Aren't you a little old for dollies?

NARRATOR: Even though Vasilisa's stepmother made her work from morning to night—and beat her if she did her work too slowly—the two stepsisters never lifted a finger. Vasilisa's father was gone so frequently that she truly had no defender left in the world.

VASILISA: *(to herself)* Oh! If my mother knew how they were treating me, she would not stand for it!

NARRATOR: Sitting sadly near the woodpile, Vasilisa pulled out her doll, stroked its braids, and stared into its eyes.

VASILISA: You are the only friend I have left in the world.

NARRATOR: Just for a second, Vasilisa thought she saw a twinkle in the doll's eye.

VASILISA: *(hopefully)* If you can hear me—please protect me from this cruel stepmother! I know she is planning to do something awful to me.

NARRATOR: The doll said nothing and looked back at her with its stitched-on smile. Vasilisa was right. Ever since the stepmother had come, she had been plotting a way to get rid of her stepdaughter for good.

STEPMOTHER: We must get rid of that awful wretch of a girl! We'll have to make it look like an accident, so her father doesn't get suspicious.

STEPSISTER ONE: Poisoning?

STEPSISTER TWO: Drowning?

STEPMOTHER: No, no! Too obvious. Ah! Wait a minute! I know!

NARRATOR: She pointed to the crackling fireplace.

STEPMOTHER: Douse that fire at once! And snuff all the candles in the house!

STEPSISTER ONE: But, Mother! Without the fire, how will we cook? We'll have no light or warmth!

STEPMOTHER: I know that! Watch while your crafty mother weaves her plan!

NARRATOR: When all the flame in the house had been extinguished, the stepmother called out to Vasilisa.

STEPMOTHER: *(sweetly)* Vasilisa, dear!

VASILISA: Yes, stepmother? If you have more chores for me to do, you will have to wait until I finish the others you have already given me.

STEPMOTHER: Don't sass me, you dirty clod! Look what has happened! The fire has gone out, and we haven't a scrap of flint or tinder. You must go fetch some fire for us!

VASILISA: Where would I go? There are no neighbors out here in the forest.

STEPMOTHER: Not so! My old auntie lives just a short distance away. I will direct you to her hut, and she will happily provide fire for you.

STEPSISTERS: *(giggling)*

VASILISA: But it's far past midday. Evening will soon fall, and it will not be safe.

STEPMOTHER: Then I guess you'll have to hurry, won't you? Stupid girl!

NARRATOR: Vasilisa realized she had no choice. The stepmother and stepsisters could barely contain their glee as she put on her shawl and scarf for the journey and secured her doll beneath her arm.

STEPMOTHER: Oh, leave that ratty, old thing behind.

VASILISA: No. It is all I have left of my *real* mother.

STEPMOTHER: They're a perfect match. It's just as lifeless as she is. Now get going before I beat you!

STEPSISTER ONE: Once you fetch the fire, we'll use that old ragdoll as kindling! *(giggles)*

NARRATOR: Vasilisa headed out of the hut into the forest. All of her circumstances seemed to tell her to despair, yet somehow she felt courage still burning in her heart.

VASILISA: *(to herself)* My stepmother thinks I will not return, but I will show her!

DOLL: *(distantly)* You are as brave as you are beautiful.

NARRATOR: Vasilisa looked down at her doll in shock. It sounded like it had spoken. Then the soft voice came again.

DOLL: I did speak, and please listen to my words. You are right. Your stepmother has sent you on an errand of death. She has sent you to Baba Yaga, the old witch who eats children. She hopes Baba Yaga will gobble you up, and then she can tell your father that you ran away. But before you go further into the forest, sneak back to your home and take five things from your kitchen: bacon, a jar of milk, cornseed, biscuits, and a bit of oil.

VASILISA: But I'm not hungry!

DOLL: They're not for eating! You will need them! Trust me!

VASILISA: How do I know I can trust you? I've never met a talking doll before.

DOLL: Your mother blessed me when she died, and now I will watch over you.

VASILISA: All right. I will trust you.

NARRATOR: So Vasilisa listened to her doll and did as it commanded her. She was good at sneaking food, for her stepmother barely fed her. Then she headed out again beneath the twisted branches of the deep wood.

VASILISA: Why shouldn't I run away and find my father?

DOLL: If you do what I tell you, all the wrongs you have suffered will be made right.

NARRATOR: Vasilisa went further and further into the forest, and the doll continued to speak to her.

DOLL: Baba Yaga flies through the air in a giant mortar bowl and uses her grinding pestle to steer. Then she sweeps away all traces of her flight with a broom.

VASILISA: What if she finds me here in the forest?

DOLL: Then she will eat you. She loves to eat children most of all. But don't worry. She usually stays in her hut during the daylight and flies out during the witching hour.

NARRATOR: Vasilisa hesitantly looked into the sky above her—partially covered by the reaching limbs of the trees. Then suddenly a rushing noise filled the forest. *(sound of horse hooves)*

VASILISA: It's her! It's Baba Yaga!

DOLL: Shhh! No! Look!

NARRATOR: A horseman appeared, dressed all in red and riding upon a red horse, and he rushed up the forest path. *(hoofbeats)* A terrible wind accompanied him, and Vasilisa, in her hiding place, felt the force of his passing. *(whooshing)* Watching him disappear into the distance, she realized that all the wood had taken on the same red hue of the rider. Sunset was approaching.

DOLL: Hurry! We must reach Baba Yaga's hut before nightfall!

NARRATOR: Vasilisa hurried on through the forest, and eventually a home appeared. At first it seemed to be a completely normal homestead. A fence surrounded a bare yard with a cottage in the midst, but then Vasilisa saw that it was truly the home of a witch. The fence was made from human bones and topped with human skulls, and the cottage stood upon two spindly chicken legs.

VASILISA: *(gasp)*

DOLL: Behold! The hut of Baba Yaga!

NARRATOR: Once again the sound of a galloping horse filled the forest behind Vasilisa. *(hoofbeats)*

VASILISA: Another horseman?

DOLL: Get down!

NARRATOR: A horseman dressed all in black and riding a black steed appeared out of the forest—rushing directly for the chicken-legged cottage. *(galloping horses hooves)* The mysterious rider jumped the bone-fence easily, the cottage spun toward the rider, exposing its doorway, and the horseman bounded directly into the open door. *(clucking of the cottage)* As Vasilisa stood blinking at this sight, she realized the world around her had gone dark. The skulls along the yard fence were glowing with eerie, blue fire.

DOLL: Are you afraid to enter now?

VASILISA: *(slowly)* Of course not. If you follow the path of fear, you will never know where to stop.

DOLL: Well-spoken, girl. Now let's enter the witch's home.

NARRATOR: Vasilisa did not like the thought of touching the bony gate, but she did, and it groaned as it opened. *(creaking of a gate)* As she stepped into the yard, she thought she heard the distant whine of a dog. *(dog growl)* She paused.

DOLL: Go on. Approach the cottage.

NARRATOR: The chicken-legged cottage had turned its doorway away from the front gate. *(clucking of a chicken)*

DOLL: *(whispering)* The cottage is bewitched and will not let you enter unless you bait it. Spread the cornseed there upon the ground.

NARRATOR: Vasilisa did as the doll commanded her to, and the cottage began to cluck hungrily. *(clucking sound)* Then it bent its knobby knees and lowered to the ground—pecking at the birdseed.

DOLL: Now! Quickly! Jump into the doorway.

NARRATOR: As the cottage door flopped open, Vasilisa jumped into it, and darkness surrounded her. She was now in the home of Baba Yaga. A room lit only by the blue flame of a fireplace was rocking violently to and fro! Odds and ends flew around the cluttered room.

BABA YAGA: *(old crone voice)* Stop! Stop you bird-brain!

NARRATOR: The room stopped rocking from side to side, and Vasilisa saw an old crone before the fire. She had gray, wiry hair, and a nose so long that it nearly touched her chin. It was Baba Yaga the witch. Baba Yaga began to grab up the cauldrons, books, and bits of flesh that had been thrown around the room.

BABA YAGA: What was I thinking? Putting chicken legs on a hut? Sure it gives you a mobile home, but look at this mess! *(pause)* I would appreciate a little help from you!

NARRATOR: At first, Vasilisa thought the witch was speaking to her. But then she noticed the largest, vilest-looking cat she had ever seen, stretched out on the table.

CAT: I would help, mistress, but I think I injured my paw during the commotion.

BABA YAGA: I'll injure more than your paw! Now get to work!

CAT: *(cat squall)* Testy. Testy.

NARRATOR: As she picked up her fallen treasures, the witch suddenly paused and sniffed with her enormous nose.

BABA YAGA: Wait! Do you smell that?

CAT: What is it? A mouse?

BABA YAGA: No, it is a child.

NARRATOR: Baba Yaga's beady eyes glittered, and sniffing sensitively, she picked her way through the clutter of the dark room.

BABA YAGA: *(sniffing)* I smell a child—but I smell no fear.

CAT: Impossible! There isn't a child living who doesn't fear you, mistress. You must be mistaken!

BABA YAGA: *(angrily)* Then I guess I'll just have to eat you for my supper instead!

CAT: Oh, but you know how you love a plump, juicy child. Especially with a few spices. Search on!

NARRATOR: Smelling her way through the darkness, the witch was very near where Vasilisa crouched. Fear was creeping up her spine, trying to paralyze her, so Vasilisa decided to do the last thing she wanted to do. She stepped forward from the shadows.

VASILISA: Looking for me?

NARRATOR: Baba Yaga could not have been more shocked!

BABA YAGA: *(shocked)* Ah! You stupid child! You ruined my game! I stalk you. I catch you. You scream. Then I eat you. *(sigh)* Oh well. Season the frying pan, cat! I guess you're off the menu for tonight.

NARRATOR: The witch's bony hand shot out and clamped on Vasilisa's wrist with incredible strength, and she began to pull her toward the fire. Vasilisa heard her doll whispering up to her frantically.

VASILISA: Wait! You cannot eat me!

BABA YAGA: Oh, yes, I can. I mean, I am trying to cut back on red meat, but…

VASILISA: Since I have shown such bravery, you must give me a task. *Then* if I do not complete that task, you may eat me. It is your way.

NARRATOR: Baba Yaga looked at the little girl fiercely, then shifted her gaze shrewdly to the doll clutched in her grip.

BABA YAGA: And just how would a little girl know a thing like that?

VASILISA: I am the daughter of a wise mother.

BABA YAGA: Fine! Fine! What does a little delay matter to me? I will give you a task, and when you do not complete it by…oh, let's say midnight, *then* I will grind your bones into bread!

CAT: Bread again? How about pudding this time?

VASILISA: But if I complete your task, you must give me some of your magic fire and allow me to leave this place.

BABA YAGA: Oh, ask anything you want, sweet-meat. There is no way you will ever complete the task I ask of you because it is so horrible, so impossible, so ghastly that no one could ever complete it. *(pause)* That's right! You must…do my laundry!

NARRATOR: There was a flash, and a mountain of grizzled undergarments filled the room.

CAT: *(shuddering)* The horror! The horror!

BABA YAGA: Oh, come off it. It's not that bad.

VASILISA: And where is the water and soap that I will use to clean all these clothes?

CAT: I would just burn them if I were you.

BABA YAGA: Shhhh! You can use this to gather water in!

NARRATOR: A sieve appeared in Vasilisa's hands. What little water collected within it drained out immediately.

BABA YAGA: Hee hee! Good luck, dearie!

CAT: Mistress, you are just *too bad!*

BABA YAGA: (*blushing*) Oh, go on!

VASILISA: Very well. When you return at midnight, you will find all your clothing neatly washed.

BABA YAGA: Hmm. Still not afraid, I see. Too bad. Fear flavors the meat. Oh well. Happy washing!

NARRATOR: Baba Yaga leapt into a giant mortar parked in a corner of the cramped room and took up her magical pestle like an oar. She pointed a knobby finger at the cat.

BABA YAGA: And if you let her escape, I'll have your hide!

CAT: You can count on me, your hideousness!

BABA YAGA: Baba Yaga! Away!

NARRATOR: Poling the bowl into motion, Baba Yaga flew out the cottage door into the black night. (*whoosh*) The cat turned to Vasilisa with a bemused look upon its face.

CAT: Heh heh. Doomed, aren't you?

VASILISA: Not really.

CAT: Is that a fact? The task that Baba Yaga gave you is impossible. I should know! I double as her maid.

VASILISA: I don't plan on completing that task.

CAT: Well, don't even think of running away. You made it into this hut easily enough, but you should know that there is a pack of bloodthirsty hounds that patrols the yard. Set one toe out the door, and they will tear the meat from your bones. And even if you happened to make it to the edge of the yard, the front gate will squeak and yell so loudly that Baba Yaga will return at once.

VASILISA: I'll take my chances.

NARRATOR: The doll whispered up to Vasilisa, and the girl nodded.

VASILISA: Cat, I appreciate all this information. In return for your kindness I would like to give you a present.

CAT: Ha! Do you think that a loyal servant like me can be bribed so easily? There is nothing in this world that would make me—(*surprised noise*) is that bacon?

NARRATOR: Vasilisa had pulled the bit of bacon from her pocket.

VASILISA: Please let me go freely, and I—

CAT: Oh yes! Go, you sweet girl, and I wish you all the luck in the world. Mmmm. Bacon! (*smacking sounds*)

NARRATOR: As the cat feasted on the bacon, Vasilisa moved toward the fireplace.

CAT: There is no way to carry that fire. But did you notice the glowing-eyed skulls when you came in? Take one of them on your way out. The same fire that burns in Baba Yaga's hearth burns in them.

NARRATOR: Vasilisa thanked the cat and turned to go.

CAT: Wait! Even if you manage to escape, Baba Yaga will catch you. Take this!

NARRATOR: The cat threw her a simple comb.

VASILISA: A comb?

CAT: A *magic* comb! If Baba Yaga chases you, throw it on the ground, and it will save you!

VASILISA: I hope your mistress does not punish you too harshly for allowing me to leave.

CAT: Who cares? I've never eaten like this in my life! All we have to eat around here is bone bread and bone pudding. I'm eternally grateful to you. I'll handle this washing for you, too.

NARRATOR: Vasilisa jumped from the front door of the chicken-legged cottage, and as soon as she did, the sound of growling dogs neared through the moonless night. (*growling dogs*)

DOLL: The biscuits! Quickly!

NARRATOR: Vasilisa threw the biscuits on the ground before the dogs, and they stared at them in wonder.

DOG: (*confused*) Huh-roo?

NARRATOR: By the time they snapped them up, Vasilisa was already to the yard gate.

DOLL: Before you open the gate, use the oil on its hinges.

NARRATOR: Vasilisa used the oil she had brought from her home. The gate swung open effortlessly.

GATE: (*relieved*) Ah! I should sound the alarm, but I've never moved so freely! My hinges feel great! Thank you!

NARRATOR: Vasilisa lifted free one of the skulls that lined the fence and carried it torch-like before her into the forest.

DOLL: Now, hurry! We must make it home before Baba Yaga returns!

VASILISA: Wait a minute! We used all of the food except the milk. What was that for?

DOLL: That is for me! I really worked up a thirst with all this advice-giving. (*slurping*)

NARRATOR: Two beams of blue light shone out from the skull, but even so, the path was hard to follow, and midnight found Vasilisa still far from home.

At midnight Baba Yaga returned home hungry, patting her bony knee in excitement. She landed her mortar and jumped free of it—smacking her cracked lips.

BABA YAGA: Where are you, morsel? Were you able to finish the laundry?

CAT: It's all neatly folded for you!

BABA YAGA: (*screaming*) What? Where is the girl? Why did you allow her to escape?

CAT: She gave me bacon! You never gave me anything half so good!

NARRATOR: Baba Yaga cursed at her servants, but they all spoke of Vasilisa's kindness.

DOG: The girl gave us biscuits! Real biscuits! You only gave us twice-gnawed bones!

GATE: She oiled my hinges! I feel ten years younger!

BABA YAGA: Worthless ingrates! I will deal with you later! I must have my dinner first!

NARRATOR: In a stormy rage Baba Yaga jumped back into her mortar and flew into the night. *(whooshing)* In the forest Vasilisa heard a rushing sound growing behind her and saw the treetops swaying.

VASILISA: *(nervously)* Doll, could that perhaps be the horseman of the dawn?

DOLL: No! This time it is Baba Yaga! Here she comes!

NARRATOR: The witch was swooping down from the sky, screaming curses so vile they cannot be spoken by human lips. Her razor-sharp fingernails were extended—seeking to claw Vasilisa's flesh.

BABA YAGA: *(yelling)*

NARRATOR: Vasilisa ran, and as she did, she threw the comb behind her. When it hit the earth, its black teeth began to grow—shooting up from the ground—becoming tall, tangled trees. *(rumbling and growing sounds)* Baba Yaga couldn't change her course quickly enough, and she flew directly into their web of limbs.

BABA YAGA: *(screaming)* Ah! Curse you! Curse you!

VASILISA: We are safe! We are safe!

DOLL: Don't stop now! Hurry on!

NARRATOR: A white rider on a white horse passed through the trees—drawing the daylight along behind him. *(hoofbeats)* By the dawning light, Vasilisa saw her family's hut in the clearing ahead, and she hurried toward it.

VASILISA: I'm home! *(sadly)* I wish I had a better home to return to.

DOLL: Oh, your journey is not done yet.

NARRATOR: Vasilisa knocked upon the door, and her stepmother jerked it open angrily.

STEPMOTHER: Yes, what is it? *(shocked)* Vasilisa?

NARRATOR: Vasilisa's stepsisters crowded in the doorway, and all of them stared at her stupefied.

STEPSISTER ONE: She survived?

STEPMOTHER: Shhhh!

STEPSISTER TWO: I thought she was supposed to—

STEPMOTHER: Yes, dear, sweet Vasilisa has returned—emptyhanded though, I'm sure.

VASILISA: No, I returned with the fire you asked of me.

STEPMOTHER: Ha! *(smugly)* Show it to me then.

VASILISA: I must warn you, it came from…

STEPMOTHER: *(angrily)* I said, show it to me!

NARRATOR: So Vasilisa raised the skull she carried in her hands. At the sight of the skull's fiery eyesockets, the faces of the stepmother and stepsisters grew pale.

STEPMOTHER: Impossible!

NARRATOR: Then the skull flew into the air and chased the stepmother and stepsisters out of the house and into the forest—gnashing its teeth behind them. *(sounds of women screaming)*

DOLL: Oh dear. It looks like they're headed in the direction of Baba Yaga's hut. Maybe she will get her meal after all.

VASILISA: Thank you, doll—for everything!

DOLL: It was your bravery that saved you, my dear—and a mother's blessing.

NARRATOR: Vasilisa's stepmother and stepsisters were never heard from again. She and her father lived a happy life, and no treasure was more precious to Vasilisa than her little doll that her mother had made just for her.

DISCUSSION QUESTIONS

1. What is strange or frightening about Baba Yaga or her household?
2. Why is Vasilisa a hero?
3. In some stories rather than being an antagonist, Baba Yaga assists heroes who come to her for help. In what ways would she make a good ally?
4. In the original version of this folktale Vasilisa's stepmother and stepsisters were burned alive when they stared into the fire of the skull's eyes. Which ending do you like better?
5. What is the theme of this story?
6. This version of the story combines two different versions of this folktale. In one version there is no magic doll. Instead Vasilisa relies on the wisdom her human aunt gives her in confronting Baba Yaga. In another version Vasilisa performs three tasks given to her by Baba Yaga with the help of her magic doll. Then Baba Yaga gives her a bit of her fire in return for successfully completing the tasks. How would these changes affect the theme of the story?

THE DEEDS OF FINN MAC COOL
TEACHER GUIDE

BACKGROUND

Celtic Mythology is brimming with heroes, gods, and magical creatures, but perhaps the most intriguing characters are the Tuatha Dé Danann, also known as the "fair folk" or the "Ever-Living Ones." The details of this supernatural race vary from source to source, but their history goes something like this: The Tuatha Dé Danann came to Erin (Ireland) as conquerors—arriving in dark clouds and using their supernatural skill to defeat the inhabitants they find there. They ruled the island for 150 years until a new race of challengers arrived: the Milesians, the ancestors of the modern Irish people. After an initial battle, the two sides agreed to a truce: They would split the land between them. The Milesians will occupy the world above while the Tuatha Dé Danann agreed to enter the sidhe (shee), the ancient burial mounds, and rule the world beneath, the Otherworld. They became the "people of the hills" or the "fairies." Over time this once mighty race, who were once initially pagan gods, became the "little people" of legend—leprechauns, fairies, and the like.

Later stories tell how the Fair Folk still come forth from their hollow hills or "fairy mounds" to cause mischief in the mortal world. Their magic makes them both wondrous and dangerous. And foolish mortals who dare venture into the Otherworld do so at their peril. Lured there by the thought of treasure and immortality, many do not return, and those who do find themselves changed forever.

SUMMARY

Two elderly women, Liath the warrior woman and Bodhmall the druidess, go into the forest to retrieve an abandoned child, the son of Cool, the leader of the Fianna warriors. They raise the boy as their own in a forest hut, protecting him from Goll the One-Eyed, the warrior who slew his father. They name him Finn, which means "fair," after his fair hair and teach him all they know.

Fourteen years pass, and finally the women sense it is time for Finn's return. First, the old women apprentice Finn to Finnegas the druid, who is attempting to catch the Salmon of Knowledge, a fish which has gained immortal wisdom from eating the magic hazelnuts that fall from a nearby tree. Finnegas catches the fish, and he instructs Finn to cook it over the fire. Yet as the fish is cooking, Finn burns his thumb and pops it into his mouth. As he does, he absorbs the salmon's wisdom. When Finnegas sees this, he realizes Finn is the rightful keeper of the salmon's wisdom and gives him the fish to eat. From this point on, whenever Finn needs a bit of wisdom, all he has to do is stick his thumb in his mouth, and wisdom will come to him. Finn sees that in order to regain his father's position among the Fianna, he must find the warriors once loyal to his father. When he does, he is reunited with his uncle who gives him a magical, crane-skin bag filled with supernatural treasures. Whenever Finn reaches into the bag, the item he needs most will be within his grasp.

Finn travels to Tara, the seat of the High King, and there announces his intent to reclaim his father's position. Goll the One-Eyed is there, and scoffs at the boy's claim. The entire court is on edge, for it is the festival of Samhain, and on this day each year Aillen the Burner, a fiend from the

Otherworld, comes out of the nearby fairy mound and burns Tara to the ground. Finn vows to defeat the fire fiend if the king will restore him to his rightful place. The king agrees.

Finn uses the magical bag and retrieves an enchanted spear head, which he affixes to a staff and waits the coming of Aillen. When Aillen arrives, he carries a fairy harp, whose song puts the entire city to sleep. Finn places the spear-head against his forehead, and its magic protects him from the enchanted harp. He then challenges Aillen and uses the spear to kill the fiend before he can use his fiery breath to set Tara ablaze. The High King restores Finn to his father's position as leader of the Fianna, and Finn agrees to make peace with Goll.

ESSENTIAL QUESTIONS

- How can knowledge aid us in our goals?
- How is reconciliation better than revenge?

ANTICIPATORY QUESTIONS

- Is gaining knowledge an important part of becoming a hero?
- Finn's patronymic is "Mac Cool" meaning "son of Cool." What would yours be? To make your own medieval Irish patronymic, add the prefix "Mac" to your father's first name.

CREATURE FEATURE

Aillen the Burner The term *fairy* may stir up images of Tinkerbell or leprechauns, but the fairies of Celtic mythology are not the "little people" of later stories. They are formidable foes like Aillen the Burner, a towering, fire-breathing fiend—an ancient deity who is angry with mortals for their role in sending his people underground.

NAME PRONUNCIATIONS

Aillen	AY-LĒN
Bodhmall	BAWD-MAHL
Fianna	FĒ-AH-NUH
Liath	LĒ-AHTH

TEACHABLE TERMS

- **Druids** were Celtic holy men, who were forbidden to write down the secrets of their religion, so very little is known about their beliefs. On pg. 89 Bodhmall the druidess teaches Finn a bit of druid lore.
- The **Fianna**, mentioned by Liath on pg. 89, were an elite group of Irish warriors who served the High King of Ireland, and there is some evidence that women served alongside the men.
- **Samhain**, which in modern Irish means "summer's end," was a yearly Celtic festival to celebrate the harvest, which eventually evolved into the modern-day tradition of Halloween. On pg. 95 Cormac references this yearly occurrence.
- The **Otherworld** (pgs. 87 and 97) is the realm of the fairies, a parallel underground dimension that can only be reached through ancient burial places or "fairy mounds."

RECALL QUESTIONS

1. What is the meaning of Finn's name?
2. How does Finn gain wisdom?
3. Crimnal gives Finn what special item?
4. Finn fights in order to prevent Aillen from doing what?
5. How does Finn withstand Aillen's spell?

THE DEEDS OF FINN MAC COOL

CAST

FINN	*Young Foundling*
BODHMALL	*Old Druid Woman*
LIATH	*Old Warrior Woman*
FINNEGAS	*Fisher Druid*
CRIMNAL	*Finn's Uncle*
GOLL	*Leader of the Fianna*
CORMAC	*High King of Erin*
SALMON	*Magical Fish*
AILLEN	*Otherworldly Creature*

NARRATOR: Deep in the wilderness of Slieve Bloom, a bundle lay nestled between the roots of a towering fir, and a pair of bright, human eyes peered between the tightly-wound blankets. An abandoned child was not an unusual sight in this forest: The fair folk were known to steal a human child away from its home or sometimes leave one of their own carelessly behind. Whether this one was from the mortal world or the Otherworld remained yet to be seen.

Soon the stillness of the forest was broken as two gray-haired, old women, one wearing the green robes of a druid priestess and the other a set of moldering armor, appeared upon the nearby pathway.

LIATH: *(old woman voice)* Give it up, Bodhmall! We've been combing these woods for hours!

BODHMALL: *(old woman voice)* No, we are close. I can feel it.

LIATH: Well, let me tell you something *I* can feel…my feet! They're killing me!

NARRATOR: The armored woman seated herself on a rock to rub her aching feet.

BODHMALL: Whatever happened to mighty Liath, "the warrior woman"?

LIATH: She got old, that's what! I've faced many a mighty foe…but none of them have come as close to defeating me as this corn on my big toe. *(grumbling)* When Lady Murne said she had a "special mission" for us, I didn't know she meant traipsing all over Slieve Bloom searching for her missing brat! Why did she leave it out here anyway? That's awfully irresponsible if you ask me!

BODHMALL: You know very well it isn't safe for her to bring the child home. Plus, she knew my second sight would lead me right to it.

LIATH: Or get us hopelessly lost. *(groaning)* Ooooh, my poor tootsies.

BODHMALL: Now, quit your grousing, so I can locate the child.

NARRATOR: Closing her eyes and placing her fingertips on her temples, Bodhmall began to hum softly. *(humming sound)*

LIATH: Okay. It's official. You've finally gone senile.

BODHMALL: *(gasp)* There it is!

NARRATOR: Bodhmall's eyes flew open, and she ran to the child, scooping it up and triumphantly displaying it to Liath.

BODHMALL: Behold! The son of Lady Murne and Cool Mac Trenmor—as promised. My second sight comes through again! What do you say now, Liath?

LIATH: I say, even a blind hog finds an acorn every once in a while. Now, let's see this baby that half the kingdom is looking for.

NARRATOR: She parted the blankets with her wrinkled fingers.

LIATH: By the gods! His hair is even whiter than ours! You know, this could be one of those…*(whispering)* fairy changelings.

BODHMALL: Nonsense. This is the child.

NARRATOR: Liath raised her spear—her eyes flitting side to side.

LIATH: That's what they want you to think! They leave their babies lying around—for bait. They're sneaky, little boogers!

BODHMALL: *(sigh)* This *is* the son of Lady Murne. And now that he is safe, we will need to build a shelter.

LIATH: *(in shock)* A shelter? What for?

BODHMALL: We're staying here in the forest. Didn't you listen to *anything* our lady said?

LIATH: Well, I heard "death-defying mission," and after that I drifted.

BODHMALL: Our mission is to keep the boy here in the woods until it is safe for him to return to the high king's court.

LIATH: Well, count me out! I'm a warrior. Not a wetnurse!

NARRATOR: Suddenly, Liath froze. The forest had suddenly gone strangely still.

LIATH: *(whispering)* Get down!

NARRATOR: The old women buried themselves in the underbrush just seconds before dark forms appeared between the trees. A grizzled, one-eyed man leading a band of warriors passed as silently as a morning mist. After they had gone, Bodhmall turned to Liath.

BODHMALL: See? That was Goll Mac Morna and his warriors! They're hunting for the baby! We must hide him and protect him at all costs.

LIATH: *(grumbling)* Fine. A month, and then I'm done! Mark my words! A month!

NARRATOR: Fourteen winters came and went. In a hidden forest glen, in a simple mud and wattle hut, the two old women raised the boy as their own. They named him "Finn," which means "fair," for his hair was as white as the barley when it ripens at harvest time.

Every evening, when the shadows grew long, Bodhmall made her way down to where the forest melted into the boglands.

There she cupped a handful of water and stared deep into it—catching glimpses of deeds far away.

BODHMALL: My second sight tells me that the world is still not safe for Finn. Although it has been fourteen years, he must stay with us a bit longer.

LIATH: Good. *(pause)* I mean...

BODHMALL: *(slyly)* What? I thought you weren't "the mothering type"?

LIATH: So what? Can't a person grow?

NARRATOR: In their secluded forest hideaway, the two old foster-mothers provided Finn the best education possible—although they did not always agree on the best method. Bodhmall taught him the wisdom of the druids—how to listen to the whispering of the leaves and find the magic in every tree and rock. Liath taught him ancient verses in praise of heroism—and how to fight and move through the underbrush as silently as a shadow. With his white-blond hair trailing long and free, Finn now stood as tall as a grown man.

LIATH: The greatest band of warriors in all of the land of Erin are called the Fianna. They're strong and fast. They live out under the trees and hunt all kinds of game. Their duty is to protect the High King and defend the borders of Erin from invaders.

FINN: And how do you know so much about the Fianna, Liath?

LIATH: I was once one of them!

FINN: But you are a woman!

LIATH: Woman or not—it doesn't matter to the Fianna. What matters is your worth!

FINN: I hope I will be worthy to join them one day.

LIATH: Then stick to your training.

NARRATOR: One evening after reading her bogwater, Bodhmall returned home down-cast.

BODHMALL: The time has come.

NARRATOR: Liath nodded and turned away to stare into the fire grimly.

FINN: What is it? You both seem so sad.

BODHMALL: It's time we told you who you really are—the real identity of your family.

FINN: *You* are my family.

BODHMALL: No, your father was Cool Mac Trenmor, the leader of the Fianna—the greatest warrior in all of Erin.

FINN: Why do you say he *was?*

LIATH: Because he was murdered by a low-down, no-good traitor named Goll the One-Eyed! Gah! Why if he were here now, I'd take care of that other eye for him!

BODHMALL: There was strife between your father's clan and Goll's clan. Goll slew your father and vowed to kill anyone still loyal to him. In fear your mother fled to the woods here—birthing you like a deer and fleeing just as quickly. She was Lady Murne the White-Necked.

FINN: So what must I do now?

LIATH: Isn't it obvious? You must go back and challenge Goll! Avenge your father! Make him Goll the No-Eyed!

NARRATOR: Finn felt so overwhelmed by all this news. Outside the hut, he could hear the leaves rustling. They seemed to be whispering some secret words to him, but he could not discern them.

FINN: I'm not ready to do such a great deed.

LIATH: What do you mean you're not ready? You're Finn Mac Cool! You've been trained for years by Liath the Warrior-Woman! What else do you need?

FINN: I will need more wisdom if I am going to challenge Goll—and win.

NARRATOR: Bodhmall smiled.

BODHMALL: You are wise, boy. There is one who lives in these woods, who could give you even more wisdom than either Liath or I ever could.

LIATH: Hmph. I doubt that.

BODHMALL: His name is Finnegas the Druid.

LIATH: *(laugh)* That crazy, old leprechaun?

FINN: Who is this Finnegas?

LIATH: Some lunatic who has been trying to catch a "magical" fish for years now. Don't waste your time with him!

BODHMALL: What do you say, Finn? Will you seek more wisdom?

NARRATOR: Finn paused thoughtfully. The whispering of the leaves seemed to be louder, more clear.

FINN: I will.

LIATH: Bah!

NARRATOR: So Finn's foster-mothers led him through the woods to the shores of the River Boyne. There on the banks, beneath an enormous hazel tree, hunched a little, old man with an enormous beard.

BODHMALL: Greetings, Finnegas!

FINNEGAS: Shhh!

NARRATOR: The little man dove into the shallow river, splashed about madly, and rose from the water, sopping wet.

FINNEGAS: You old biddies just cost me the catch of a lifetime! I had that fish right where I wanted him!

NARRATOR: Liath leveled her spear into the little man's face.

LIATH: Call me a "biddy" again, you old rootwad, and I'll slice those whiskers right off your face!

BODHMALL: Forgive us for interrupting your work, Finnegas, but we come in peace. We have brought our young ward to you—to be apprenticed.

NARRATOR: Finnegas crawled out of the riverbed without giving Finn a second look.

FINNEGAS: No way! The last thing I need around here is some overgrown brat.

NARRATOR: Stepping forward earnestly, Finn bowed before the old druid.

FINN: Sir, I am Finn Mac Cool, the rightful son of one of Erin's greatest warriors. I need your wisdom to win my rightful place among the Fianna and restore honor to my family name.

NARRATOR: Finnegas stared at Finn with a look of amusement.

FINNEGAS: Verbal, isn't he?

FINN: Wise druid, what is it that you seek here in this river?

FINNEGAS: Well, since you asked so politely—for seven years I've tried to catch the Salmon of Knowledge that swims in these waters. Yet he has eluded me time and time again.

LIATH: Have you tried the Turtle of Insanity? That might be more your speed.

FINN: How could a fish give you wisdom?

FINNEGAS: The Salmon was not always so wise. For centuries it has fed from the hazelnuts that fall from this enchanted tree and has become wiser than any other creature on earth.

LIATH: Ha! I say that's just a regular, old fish, and you're a crazy, old leprechaun.

NARRATOR: Just then the face of a red-speckled fish poked itself above the surface of the river.

SALMON: Actually, Finnegas is right. I'm incredibly intelligent.

LIATH: Ah! A talking fish! Kill it!

FINNEGAS: *(crazily)* See! See how it taunts me? Now get out of here, all of you! I have some fishing to do!

NARRATOR: Bodhmall neared the old man with a shrewd look upon her face.

BODHMALL: What if I told you the only way that this fish will ever be caught is if you take Finn to be your apprentice?

FINNEGAS: And how would you know that?

LIATH: She sees things…in her magical pond scum.

NARRATOR: Finnegas sucked one of his teeth shrewdly.

FINNEGAS: Fine! The boy can stay! But once I have caught the fish, he's gone.

FINN: And you promise to train me in all that you know?

LIATH: That won't take long.

FINNEGAS: Yes, yes.

NARRATOR: Finn stood and embraced his old foster-mothers fondly.

FINN: Then I guess this is goodbye. I shall miss you.

BODHMALL: I will watch your progress from afar.

LIATH: Remember—we feel responsible for you. Don't embarrass us. *(sniffing)*

FINN: Liath? Are you crying?

LIATH: No, I just got a bit of hazelnut in my eye.

NARRATOR: So the two old women tearfully departed—leaving Finn, the boy they had raised up from a babe, alone with the fisher-druid.

FINN: So, Master Finnegas, what will you do with unlimited knowledge?

FINNEGAS: For starters, not answer stupid questions! The fish's wisdom makes him too wily to catch. I've tried spears and nets and even a bit of magic, but he eludes me every time.

SALMON: Perhaps if you didn't speak your plans out loud they would be more effective.

NARRATOR: The fish's smiling face had reappeared in the river shallows.

FINNEGAS: *(cries of anger)* Arg! He tasks me! He heaps me!

FINN: Here. Maybe I could try.

FINNEGAS: *(sarcastically)* Oh yes! I'm sure that some ignorant boy is going to succeed where, I, a fisher-druid, have failed for years!

FINN: I think I have him on the line.

NARRATOR: The druid blinked in astonishment. Sure enough, Finn was dangling a line into the water—with the salmon's lips clamped firmly onto the other end.

FINNEGAS: How did—? Nevermind! Don't move! I'll be right back with the net.

(joyfully) Wah-hoo! Unlimited knowledge! Mine! All mine!

NARRATOR: As the old druid skipped away to retrieve his net, Finn stared down into the salmon's wise, watery eyes.

SALMON: Greetings, Finn Mac Cool. I have been waiting for you. And now that you are here, I am allowing myself to be caught.

FINN: I thank you for your kindness. If you give Finnegas your knowledge, he will share it with me.

SALMON: He who seeks knowledge for its own good will gain even more.

NARRATOR: When Finnegas returned, they hauled the fish out of the river as the old druid gloated over his longtime adversary.

FINNEGAS: Who is the wise one now, you scaly scalawag? All right, boy, prepare a fire!

SALMON: Farewell, Finn Mac Cool! Use my knowledge well.

NARRATOR: So they skinned the fish and placed its flesh on a spit over a roaring fire.

FINNEGAS: *(yawn)* I'm going to lie down for a bit. You finish cooking the fish, but don't you dare eat a bit of it!

FINN: Of course not, master.

NARRATOR: Finn continued to turn the fish over the fire, but as he did so, he happened to touch its cooking flesh. This burned his thumb, which he quickly stuck into his mouth. At once, torrents of secret knowledge flooded his mind. *(sound of knowledge flooding Finn's mind)*

FINNEGAS: *(waking up sound)* All right! It should be cooked by now. *(pause)* Wait a minute. What has happened?

NARRATOR: Finnegas stared into Finn's eyes with a wild, searching look.

FINNEGAS: *(angrily)* I can see it! You have absorbed the salmon's knowledge!

FINN: How? All I did was suck on my burnt finger!

FINNEGAS: *(sigh)* It's too late! The gods have spoken! This fish was not meant for me! It was meant for you. Fine. Go ahead. Eat it. It's yours.

NARRATOR: Against the pleading of Finn, Finnegas forced him to eat the entirety of the fish. Even more knowledge flooded his mind, yet the most concentrated spot was still his thumb. From that day forward, whenever he need a bit of knowledge, he would place his thumb between his teeth, and any knowledge he sought would come to him.

FINNEGAS: Now, you must journey on, boy. Face your destiny. Use the knowledge to achieve your rightful place.

NARRATOR: So Finn departed the River Boyne. Unsure of where to journey next, he placed his thumb in his mouth and bit down upon it. Sure enough, a sudden vision flooded his mind: the misty image of gray-haired men camped upon a mountain slope.

FINN: These are the warriors who were once loyal to my father. Goll the One-Eyed has driven them into exile. Perhaps the key to my destiny lies with them.

NARRATOR: Finn journeyed through the mountains until he saw the men's campfires through the trees. When he stepped from the forest shadows, appearing like a ghost in their midst, the gray-haired warriors grabbed up their weapons. *(shouts of confusion)*

CRIMNAL: *(yelling)* Halt! Who are you? If you are friend, prove it quickly, or you will forfeit your life!

FINN: I am a friend, but the only proof I have is my name. I am Finn Mac Cool.

CRIMNAL: No! It can't be!

NARRATOR: The leader of the gray warriors drew forward and squinted into the boy's face.

CRIMNAL: It's true! I can see your father in you. I am Crimnal, Cool's brother—your very own uncle.

NARRATOR: The exiled Fianna welcomed Finn warmly, and they spent many hours around the fire—speaking of the past. They rejoiced when Finn spoke of his quest to restore honor to the Fianna.

CRIMNAL: That villainous Goll and all of Clan Morna drove us into exile here. We are dishonored, but if you would plead our case to the High King, I'm sure he would restore us.

FINN: I promise to do all in my power to make it so.

CRIMNAL: Good. Then you will need this.

NARRATOR: Crimnal held out a bag made from the skin of a crane.

CRIMNAL: It may look simple, but it contains magical items from the fairy world—treasures collected from generations of adventures. Goll tried to steal it way, but it belongs to you, the rightful leader of the Fianna. When you reach inside, the object you most desperately need will appear within your grasp.

NARRATOR: Finn reached into the bag, but when he withdrew his hand, it was empty.

CRIMNAL: Don't worry. You have all you need now, but when the time comes for you to face Goll in mortal combat and avenge the death of your father, the bag will aid you.

FINN: Must I kill a man whom I've never met?

CRIMNAL: It is the way.

FINN: But is it the only way?

NARRATOR: The time came for Finn to depart, and Crimnal offered to accompany him to Tara, the seat of the High King, but Finn declined.

FINN: It would only mean danger for you.

NARRATOR: Finn belted the crane-skinned bag around his waist and bid his father's comrades goodbye.

Finn traveled on to Tara, where he found the royal city's gates shut and bolted against all visitors. The guards upon the city walls accosted him, and Finn was ushered to stand at last before the High King, Cormac Mac Art.

CORMAC: Who are you, stranger? Your face is not familiar to me.

FINN: I am just a simple traveler.

NARRATOR: Beside the king's throne sat a grizzled warrior who could only be Goll—his empty eye-socket glaring at the boy grimly.

GOLL: (*growling*) Don't lie to us, boy! I may have one eye, but I see better than most men.

FINN: Then you should have noticed that I am Finn the son of Cool, who was once rightful leader of the Fianna.

(*gasping from the hall*)

CORMAC: (*happily*) Boy! You are most welcome! Your father was one of my most trusted Fianna warriors!

FINN: I have come here to serve you, my king, but not to join the Fianna. I have heard that their leader is less-than-worthy.

GOLL: Why you little—! Your father was a villain. His clan took my eye!

FINN: So you took his life? Where is the honor in that? You brought division to the Fianna, a true brotherhood of warriors. You are a sower of discord, and anyone who doesn't see that is blinder than you are.

NARRATOR: Goll drew his sword. (*Shing!*)

CORMAC: Lower your weapon, Goll! This boy may stay—and under my protection. This feuding among the Fianna must end.

GOLL: *(angrily)* It will end—when this young pup is dead!

NARRATOR: Suddenly, a phantom gust of wind blew through the hall—snuffing out each and every torch. *(whooshing)* A ghostly laughter echoed in the darkness. *(ghoulish laughter)* The king quickly ordered the torches relit—revealing every face white with fear. Finn looked to the king in shock.

CORMAC: This is the night of Samhain, when the barrier between the fairy world and our world grows thin. For the past nine years, a terror has come out of the hollow hills nearby—to torture us. Aillen the Burner, he is called.

FINN: Then he is one of the Tuatha Dé Danaan, the people of the hills—the immortal race who agreed to live underground ages ago.

CORMAC: Impressive! You know much of the old lore for one so young. Yes, he is one of the fair folk, but in spite of the peace between our peoples, the Burner brings his anger against us year after year.

FINN: But why do none of your *brave* warriors face this creature?

GOLL: Ha! What chance does a warrior of flesh and blood have against a fiend from the fairy world?

FINN: Plenty—if he is not a coward.

GOLL: *(angrily)* That's it!

CORMAC: Silence, Goll! *(continuing)* Each year I offer gold and riches to any warrior brave enough to face the creature. But I have given up all hope.

FINN: I will rid your kingdom of this creature if you grant me a request: Make me the leader of the Fianna. Let me take my father's place.

NARRATOR: Goll shot the king a frenzied look, but Cormac simply stroked his beard.

CORMAC: I will gladly…if you achieve such a feat. Goll, will you swear loyalty to this boy if he succeeds?

GOLL: *(sarcastically)* Oh, of course, your majesty! I will also marry the queen of the fairies when she comes to court me.

CORMAC: I would not joke of it, Goll. I myself have been in the realm of the fairies. They lured me there to teach me a bit of wisdom, and I returned with many treasures. One is this very cup.

NARRATOR: The High King held up what appeared to be a simple cup.

CORMAC: Whoever holds it must speak the truth, or it will break into pieces.

NARRATOR: He handed the cup to Goll.

CORMAC: Do you swear to put aside this feud and serve the boy if he succeeds?

NARRATOR: Goll's eye darted from his warriors, to his king, and finally to Finn, his adversary.

GOLL: *(coldly)* I swear.

NARRATOR: The cup remained intact.

GOLL: But no man can defeat such a creature—especially not some orphaned brat!

NARRATOR: At these words the cup broke apart into three pieces. *(cracking sound)*

CORMAC: Bring me the pieces of the cup. Whenever someone holds them and speaks the truth, they reform. I say, no man here can match your bravery, Finn Mac Cool.

NARRATOR: The cup reformed within the king's hand.

CORMAC: Now, son of Cool, go and prepare yourself for battle.

NARRATOR: Finn began to leave the hall, but Goll hissed at him.

GOLL: *(hissing)* When you return in defeat, I will be waiting here to end your life.

FINN: Is that any way to speak to your future leader?

NARRATOR: Entering the night air, Finn climbed and stood upon the city walls. He placed his thumb between his teeth, and a vision sprang into his mind—a dark form the size of a tree with blazing eyes, its fingers plucking the strings of a glistening harp. As the notes fell to the earth, every living creature succumbed to sleep beneath the melody.

FINN: That is how the Burner does it. He puts everyone in Tara asleep before burning the city to the ground. But how do I stop him?

NARRATOR: Another image formed in his mind—a spinning triangle—a spearhead enchanted with fairy magic and forged by the smith of the gods. Beside it appeared a finely-crafted cloak—its hues as green as the living forest. Finn knew what he must do. He opened the bag slung at his hip, envisioning the spearhead and the cloak, and reached inside. His hand sunk far into the bag—far deeper than he expected. Then his fingers felt the metallic smoothness of the spearhead and the softness of the cloak, and he drew them out.

FINN: The only way to fight fairy magic is with fairy magic.

NARRATOR: He attached the spearhead onto the end of a shaft and slung the regal cloak about his shoulders. Then he waited. The noise of the feasting died down, and the noises of the night filled the air. *(cricket sounds)* By imperceptible degrees the air grew deathly still, and a mist floated out of the hills, engulfing the city. Finn thought he heard faraway notes, but this did not alarm him. *(strange music)* The music was soothing, comforting. His eyelids were growing heavy, terribly heavy—like lead—and then they fell shut.

FINN: No!

NARRATOR: Finn touched the enchanted spearhead to his brow, raging fury flowed from it, and his eyes flew open. The city around him had succumbed to supernatural slumber.

Then he saw it. Something tall and dark was moving through the mists—stepping between the shadows. Its branch-like arms almost dragged the ground, and light poured out of its furnace-like mouth. It was Aillen the Burner.

AILLEN: *(mystically)* Tara! Tara! Seat of the high king. Tonight I come to destroy you yet again! Long ago, your people drove my people underground. But I have returned, as the champion of my kin, bent on revenge. Sleep. Sleep. Listen to my song and sleep.

NARRATOR: In the dark fairy's grip was clutched an enchanted harp—his long fingers plucking at its strings. Finn sprang toward the fiend, his spear at the ready.

FINN: Halt! There is still one man who has not fallen prey to your spell!

AILLEN: (*growling*) Impossible! No one can withstand my magic!

FINN: Put away your anger! Your people rule below. We rule above. Let there be peace between us!

AILLEN: Peace? (*eerie laughter*) I will never rest until your race crumbles into ash!

FINN: Then if there cannot be peace, I will defend my people.

AILLEN: No. You will die!

NARRATOR: Aillen roared, and fire blazed forth from his open mouth in a wave of heat. (*whooshing of flame*) The column of fire fell upon Finn—enveloping him completely.

AILLEN: Hmph. Measly mortal. You were foolish to challenge me.

NARRATOR: Turning away from his conquered foe, Aillen aimed his fiery breath toward the walls of Tara. Yet Finn rose up from beneath his magical cloak unscathed.

AILLEN: It can't be!

FINN: I am Finn Mac Cool! I am cloaked and armed with treasures of your people. You cannot defeat me, and now I will deal you your death.

NARRATOR: Fear came into the fire-fiend's glowing eyes, and he fled—taking great, running leaps back toward his fairy mound. The dark hillside opened like a gateway—green light pouring forth from the Otherworld. Aillen had almost reached the threshold when Finn sent his spear singing through the air. (*Shunk!*) It pierced the fairy's body, and with splutters of flame, he fell to the ground.

AILLEN: (*fading away*) No! No! No!

NARRATOR: Finn approached the spot where Aillen had fallen. All that remained of the fire-fiend was a twisted corpse of vines and heather grass. Finn decapitated the terror, slung the head over his shoulder, and carried it back within the walls of Tara. In the High King's throne room, he found the entire court fast asleep in their places.

FINN: (*loudly*) Awake!

NARRATOR: Finn slammed the Aillen's head down upon the table before the king and his court, and they sprang back to life.

FINN: Awaken, my king! This enemy will trouble you no longer.

CORMAC: My boy! You have done it! You have defeated the demon!

NARRATOR: Even Goll's one eye glimmered with admiration. Finn turned to face his familial foe.

FINN: Now I ask you, Goll—will you keep your oath? Will you serve me faithfully? If so, I will forget all the blood between your clan and mine.

GOLL: (*slowly*) I will.

NARRATOR: Goll stuck out his hand and clasped Finn's, and all those gathered there let up a mighty cheer. *(loud cheering)*

From that day on, Finn Mac Cool led the Fianna with fairness and wisdom and became their greatest leader. These were just the first of the mighty deeds of Finn Mac Cool, who went on to win fame and valor in the world of men and the world beyond.

DISCUSSION QUESTIONS

1. What makes Finn a hero?
2. How does magic play a large part in Finn's success?
3. Finn decides to seek knowledge before facing his father's enemy. How does this benefit him?
4. Is Finn wise to make peace with Goll, his longtime enemy?
5. Compare Aillen the Burner and Finn. How is their response to revenge different?
6. The Fianna were a real group of warriors who served the king of Ireland. Some records show that women were included among this group. How does Liath, the warrior woman, help prepare Finn for his quest?
7. Druids were Celtic holy men. Since they were forbidden to write down the details of their beliefs and all of their lore was passed orally, very little is known about their religion. How does Bodhmall the druidess help prepare Finn for his quest?
8. Many Irish stories feature humans who foolishly enter the realm of the fairies. Some become enchanted by the fairy music and dance there for eternity. Some return after only a few days in the Otherworld to find that years have passed in their absence. If you had a chance to enter a magical world, would you take it? Explain.
9. There is a theory that the fair folk or the "people of the hills" were originally the pagan gods of the Celts. Over time, they shrank in stature until they became fairies and leprechauns, mischief makers instead of powerful deities. How is this reflected in the story?
10. Later Irish stories continue the life of Finn Mac Cool. When Finn grows to manhood, he soon finds love. One day, Finn's hounds capture a deer in the forest. To his astonishment, it magically transforms into a beautiful woman named Sadb. Explaining she has been changed into that form for refusing the love of a druid, she and Finn soon fall in love and marry. Eventually, she bears him a son named Oisin ("little fawn"), who grows up to be a bard and adventurer almost as famous as his father. Do these later adventures in the life of Finn complement those of his early years?

GRANDFATHER CHENOO
TEACHER GUIDE

BACKGROUND

Skeletal woodwalkers that haunt the frozen landscape of North America, Chenoo are some of folklore's most terrifying mythological creatures. Cursed into their monstrous form by eating human flesh, the Chenoo originate with the Algonquin people of eastern Canada. Such a strong warning against cannibalism seems only natural in hunter-gather societies who dwelt in areas where prolonged winters sometimes led to starvation. The horrific tales of the Chenoo (and other similar creatures like the infamous Wendigo) helped define the boundaries of what was acceptable conduct. Within these cultures Chenoo serve as a warning: No matter how hungry one becomes, it is better to starve than to eat the flesh of another.

The Chenoo's appearance accentuates their symbolic monstrousness. Chenoo have a bony figure, akin to humans on the verge of starvation. In fact, most of them have chewed their lips off in hunger. They are said to have frozen, human-shaped hearts. The Chenoo can change their size—growing from human height to as tall as the trees—and are closely associated with winter. All these details combine to make them the walking embodiment of horror.

SUMMARY

Nesoowa and Toma, her husband, travel into the hostile North Woods, where they plan to make a new home. As they travel, an old woman warns them of journeying any further northward since the woods ahead are filled with creatures called Chenoo, former humans who became monsters after eating human flesh. Ignoring her warning, Nesoowa and Toma build their new home in the North Woods.

One day later when Toma is away hunting, Nesoowa encounters a Chenoo—bone thin and its lips gnawed off by its own razor-sharp teeth. Knowing that she has no chance of escape, Nesoowa treats the Chenoo kindly, even referring to him as "Grandfather." This confuses the Chenoo, and Nesoowa leads him back to her lodge and hosts him as a beloved family member. When Toma returns home to find the deadly creature in their lodge, Nesoowa urges him to go along with the charade since it has kept the Chenoo from attacking.

Days pass, and the Chenoo continues to live with the young couple. Nesoowa begins to wonder if it is possible for the creature to turn good again. A talking crow appears at their wigwam and tells them not to trust the Chenoo. The crow has witnessed a battle between this Chenoo and a larger one and claims the Chenoo is simply biding its time until it regains its strength. Then it will attack.

Nesoowa continues to hope though, and one day the Chenoo speaks, asking her to boil some moose fat for it to drink. The Chenoo tells the couple that his name is Elaak, and a larger Chenoo named Winsit is searching for him. Elaak hopes to defeat this Chenoo and eat its heart, which is how he will become even more powerful. As their strange family relationship continues, Elaak takes Toma hunting and kills a giant lizard.

One day the crow brings word that Winsit has discovered Elaak's hiding place and is coming to kill him. Elaak gives Nesoowa two golden horns and tells her to drive them into the ear of Winsit if he kills Elaak. Then Elaak tells the couple to hide in a cave and plug their ears with moss, or the war-cry of the giant Chenoo will kill them instantly.

Nesoowa prays for a way to save Elaak, and a jaybird sent by the heavenly protector, Glooscap, shows her a special flower that if ingested by Elaak will return him to human form. Nesoowa and Toma run to where the two Chenoo are battling. Toma jabs one of the golden horns into Winsit's ear and kills him. Then Nesoowa offers a drink containing the special flower to Elaak. When Elaak drinks the potion, he vomits up a human-shaped block of ice and returns to his human form. He spends the rest of his days living with Toma and Nesoowa.

ESSENTIAL QUESTIONS

- Is redemption possible for everyone?
- Can love defeat fear?

ANTICIPATORY QUESTIONS

- What is cannibalism?
- What do you think a Chenoo is? Answer before and after you look at the illustration.

NAME PRONUNCIATIONS

Nesoowa	NEH-SOO-WAH
Toma	TŌ-MUH
Chenoo	CHĒ-NOO
Winsit	WINS-IT
Kaka-kooch	KAH-KUH-KOOCH
Glooscap	GLOOS-CAP

CREATURE FEATURE

Chenoo Creatures that were once human, Chenoo become monsters by devouring the flesh of a fellow human being. Once in this form, no human weapon can kill them. Using their magical powers, Chenoo can become as large as trees. From that point on, they gain more power by devouring the hearts of fellow Chenoo. The Chenoo shares many interesting similarities with another American Indian monster: the Wendigo.

TEACHABLE TERMS

- **Foreshadowing** On pgs. 101-102 the old woman warns Nesoowa and Toma of the dangers of the north woods, foreshadowing their encounter with the Chenoo.
- **Motif: Talking Animals** American Indian tales often feature animals who can freely converse with humans. The crow and jaybird in this myth are two examples of this motif.
- **Metaphor** With their terrifying, ever-hungry nature Chenoo are a living metaphor for the crime of cannibalism.
- **Allusion** On pg. 109 Nesoowa mentions Glooscap (also known as Gluscabi), a hero of the Wabanaki peoples who uses his divine powers to protect the world.
- **Symbol** On pg. 111 the melting of the Chenoo's frozen heart is symbolic of shedding his monstrous qualities.
- **Theme** The heart of this myth is the theme of love overcoming hatred.

RECALL QUESTIONS

1. How does a human turn into a Chenoo?
2. How does Nesoowa react when she meets a Chenoo?
3. What weapon does the Chenoo give to Toma?
4. What secret does a jaybird tell Nesoowa?
5. After Elaak's victory over Winsit, what does Nesoowa do?

GRANDFATHER CHENOO

CAST

NESOOWA	*Young Wife*
TOMA	*Young Husband*
CHENOO	*Woodland Monster*
WINSIT	*Chenoo Monster*
WOMAN	*Elderly Traveler*
CROW	*Black Bird*
JAY	*Small Bird*

NARRATOR: In the Old Time when the world was much different, a young beauty named Nesoowa married a brave hunter named Toma. The couple loved the village in which they lived, but they longed for adventure, so together they decided to journey to a new life in the lonely North Woods, where the land was wilder and still filled with mystery.

With their meager belongings strapped on their backs, the couple traveled the forest paths northward. As they did, they passed fewer and fewer settlements until all traces of human life vanished, and the towering firs and spruces seemed to blot out the sun.

TOMA: Well, we have done it, Nesoowa. We have traveled so far that we have left all civilization behind.

NESOOWA: I will miss our families, but I am glad that we can have this new adventure together.

NARRATOR: One day as they continued northward, the couple was surprised to meet a solitary traveler—a haggard, old woman—stumbling along the path. When she noticed Toma and Nesoowa, she sucked in her breath and drew back as if she had seen a ghost.

WOMAN: *(gasp)* Who are you?

NARRATOR: Toma addressed the old woman respectfully.

TOMA: Hello, Grandmother. We mean you no harm. We are traveling further into the North Woods.

WOMAN: That is not a place for humans to live. Only the Chenoo live there.

NESOOWA: Chenoo?

WOMAN: Wood-walkers! Creatures that feed on human flesh and fill their bodies with dark magic. They can grow as tall as a tree, and no other creature can kill them.

NARRATOR: Toma smiled kindly at the woman.

TOMA: Really, Grandmother? And where do these creatures come from?

WOMAN: Stupid boy! Don't you know? They were once human, but starvation drove them to eat the flesh of their fellow man. Then their hearts froze, and they became Chenoo.

NESOOWA: We are not afraid, Grandmother. My husband here is a mighty hunter!

NARRATOR: Toma swelled with pride at his wife's compliment.

WOMAN: Ha! Nothing can hunt a Chenoo. They hunt *us*. The North Woods is not a place to live. It is a place to die.

NARRATOR: Then the old woman pushed past them and hurried on down the path.

TOMA: Strange woman.

NESOOWA: Must be one of *your* long-lost relatives.

NARRATOR: The happy couple shrugged off the old woman's warnings and continued northward until they found a spot in the deep woods just perfect for their new life together.

TOMA: I like it here. It will be wild and free.

NESOOWA: You go and hunt each day, and when you bring home a kill, I will cook it up into a tasty meal.

NARRATOR: Even as Toma and Nesoowa smiled to one another, a chilly wind blew through the trees and caused them to draw their fur coats closer about them.

Their first days in the North Woods were spent building themselves a warm wigwam lodge. As they pulled loose pieces of the underbrush, a noisy bird flew out from the thicket.

CROW: *(crow squawking)* Che-noo! Che-noo!

NESOOWA: Listen to that bird! He is saying Chenoo!

TOMA: It's just your imagination.

NARRATOR: As the bird disappeared into the distance, Nesoowa and Toma noticed that all other sounds from the forest had gone silent. No insect chirped. No leaf rustled. Then between the tops of the towering firs, they saw something moving.

TOMA: Nesoowa, get down!

NARRATOR: Toma drew his bow and aimed it toward the tall, shadowy form moving through the firs. *(whispering of the trees)* A thousand, ghostly whispers accompanied the shadow's passing. And then it was gone.

NESOOWA: *(frightened)* You saw it, didn't you? It was big as a tree!

TOMA: Probably just a shadow passing across the sun.

NARRATOR: As winter arrived, Toma went to hunt daily, returning with mighty kills, but his hunting trips took him farther and farther away from the lodge.

Nesoowa spent many days alone. One still, frigid day when she had gone down to the river's edge to draw water, she felt an unimaginable coldness seize her—as if her body had never known warmth.

NESOOWA: *(gasp)*

NARRATOR: Standing silently near her was a tall, gaunt form—its skin pale and its eyes wolf-like. Icicles dangled from its brow, and its lips had been gnawed away by its own needle-like teeth. Its fingers, which were long and sharp, were twitching with hunger. She knew instantly it was a Chenoo, and she was its prey.

CHENOO: *(hissing)* Hssssss.

NARRATOR: Toma was miles away, and besides Nesoowa knew that no manmade weapon was able to harm a Chenoo. There was nothing between her and death—except her quick wits. The muscles of the Chenoo tensed—ready to spring. Nesoowa's instinct was to run, but instead a soft inspiration spoke to her heart. She advanced toward the monster—her face beaming with joy.

NESOOWA: *(happily)* Grandfather! There you are!

NARRATOR: The Chenoo's yellow eyes opened widely, and it looked side to side. Was this girl addressing it?

NESOOWA: Grandfather, we haven't seen you in ages. Where have you been?

NARRATOR: The Chenoo had witnessed all kinds of reactions from its victims. Some had shrieked their minds out, and others had wept for mercy. Yet this strange reaction puzzled it, and the monster that could kill in an instant paused. Nesoowa grabbed the monster's death-cold hand. It sent a stinging chill throughout her entire body, but she held on. Then she led the creature back toward her lodge.

NESOOWA: You look absolutely awful, Grandfather. I will have to give you some of my husband's clothes to wear.

NARRATOR: The Chenoo did look haggard. Its hair was hanging from its head in long, white wisps, and she could tell it was starving—as it always was. Around its mouth was a ring of crusted blood—the only remnant of its lips. The monster's right side was shredded, too—just below its pronounced ribcage.

NESOOWA: You are wounded!

NARRATOR: Nesoowa reached out to touch the wound.

CHENOO: *(snarling and hissing)* Hiss!

NARRATOR: Nesoowa, growing more confident, snapped back.

NESOOWA: *(scolding)* Quiet now! Don't bark at me because you got yourself hurt! And don't you dare come inside our lodge without first going to the river to wash up!

NARRATOR: The monster narrowed its evil eyes to slits.

NESOOWA: To the river! At once!

NARRATOR: Surprisingly, the Chenoo did as the young woman commanded and padded back down the snowy pathway to the river.

NESOOWA: *(to herself)* I can't believe that worked! What now? Can I really invite a man-eating monster into my home?

NARRATOR: She noticed a crow was perched on the edge of the lodge roof.

CROW: Che-noo! Che-noo!

NESOOWA: Now you tell me! *(pause)* Okay, I must think quickly. Toma is miles away. My only hope will be to entertain the Chenoo until he returns. Maybe then we can make an escape.

NARRATOR: Soon the Chenoo returned to the wigwam. Its side had been washed. Nesoowa clothed it in some of her husband's garments. She built up the fire, but the Chenoo shrank back from it angrily—its face full of hatred.

NESOOWA: Oh, that's right, Grandfather. I forgot that you prefer the cold. Just sit by the wigwam's flap, and we'll leave that open for you. I prefer the heat myself.

NARRATOR: She offered the Chenoo some food, and it only hissed at the offer.

CHENOO: *(hissing)* Hsssss.

NESOOWA: Fine! Suit yourself. Keep gnawing your lips off. See if I care!

NARRATOR: Ignoring the Chenoo's demonic gaze from across the fire, Nesoowa busied herself. She knew that Toma would soon return home, and she needed a way to warn him of the Chenoo's presence.

NESOOWA: Grandfather, I must go and chop some wood. I will be back soon.

NARRATOR: But the Chenoo rose and followed her out of the lodge.

NESOOWA: *(to herself)* This is it. Now he will kill me.

NARRATOR: Nesoowa grabbed up the axe and turned to face the Chenoo. It reached its long, bony hands out and took the axe out of her hands. Nesoowa closed her eyes—waiting for death to take her. But the Chenoo simply walked past her and went to work with blazing speed—chopping tree after tree down into firewood. *(sounds of chopping)* It returned and threw the axe down at her feet with a grunt.

CHENOO: *(grunt)* Hrmmm.

NARRATOR: Nesoowa stood amazed. Just then she heard a call from the woods. *(faraway call)* It was Toma returning from the hunt. Her husband walked into the clearing and stopped dead in his tracks—staring at the sight of his wife standing next to a Chenoo—one dressed in his own clothing.

TOMA: *(stammering)* It's—it's…

NARRATOR: Nesoowa jumped forward.

NESOOWA: Yes! It's our grandfather! He has come to stay with us! Isn't that wonderful?

TOMA: *(barely able to speak)* Yes…wonderful…

NARRATOR: Nesoowa flashed Toma a "trust me" expression.

TOMA: It's good to see you…Grandfather.

NESOOWA: Grandfather, you remember Toma, right?

CHENOO: *(dubious grunting)* Hrrmmm.

NESOOWA: Toma, tell Grandfather all about your hunt while I prepare the evening meal.

TOMA: Uh...

NARRATOR: Nesoowa shooed her husband and the monster inside, and Toma soon fell in with the deception. His words filled the lodge as the Chenoo stared at him over the fire. Nesoowa offered the Chenoo tobacco and finally a hot meal, but it refused both. Finally, the Chenoo's head began to nod, and it fell asleep.

TOMA: *(whispering)* Nesoowa, what are we going to do? We have a Chenoo in our home!

NESOOWA: *(whispering)* I did the only thing I knew to do!

TOMA: It has saved our lives for now, but that thing is a monster. Tomorrow it will eat us for sure!

CROW: You can be sure about that!

NARRATOR: They looked at one another in shock. Who had spoken? Up in the darkness of the lodge sat a crow—picking at its feathers.

NESOOWA: You spoke!

CROW: I've spoken to you before!

NESOOWA: All you said was "Chenoo! Chenoo!"

CROW: What else did I need to say, you dumb human? I tried to warn you, but did you listen? No!

TOMA: Keep your voice down!

CROW: Fine! I won't tell you all I know about that Chenoo.

NESOOWA: Fine, brother crow. Tell us about the Chenoo. But quietly—and quickly before it awakens.

CROW: You wanna know how that Chenoo got wounded? I saw it all. It grew as tall as a tree and battled a bigger, badder Chenoo. Chenoo are thick in these parts. That's why we don't see many of your kind around here. During the battle, your Chenoo was nearly killed. That's the only reason it hasn't killed *you*...yet.

TOMA: Then why don't you make yourself useful and tell us how to escape?

CROW: Escape? Impossible! You're completely at that thing's mercy. Even in a weakened state, Chenoo are still deadly. If you tried to run, it would be upon you. They can skeletize a human in a minute flat. I've seen it!

NESOOWA: But Chenoo were once human, right? Can't they turn human again?

CROW: Impossible! It has a heart of ice. Nothing can change it back now. Keeping it here will allow it to grow stronger, and then it will eat you both.

TOMA: Then if there is no hope, leave us in peace!

CROW: Fine! That's gratitude for you! *(crow sounds)*

NARRATOR: The crow took wing and flew out the lodge doorway. Toma and Nesoowa settled down by the fire and clung to each other all night—sure that any moment they would feel the bloody claws of the monster tearing at their flesh. But when morning came, the Chenoo rose from sleep—its features still grim and its gaze hateful.

NESOOWA: Good morning, Grandfather. Would you care for some breakfast?

CHENOO: *(negative sound)* Psstt!

NESOOWA: You're skin and bone! You should eat *something*.

TOMA: *(through his teeth)* Don't encourage it.

NESOOWA: Toma must go and hunt, Grandfather, but you and I will stay here.

TOMA: *(whispering)* Nesoowa, I refuse to leave you here!

NESOOWA: Nothing will harm me, husband. I have my dear Grandfather to protect me.

NARRATOR: She patted the bony hand of the monster, who looked back at her with a mixture of hatred and confusion. Toma did not wish to go, but a stern look from Nesoowa sent him out the door.

Toma feared the worst, but when he returned, he found his wife and the Chenoo just as he had left them.

NESOOWA: Well, look, Grandfather! Toma has returned—and with such a fine kill, too! Perhaps you will share a bit of stew with us?

CHENOO: Blah!

NARRATOR: Days passed, and every day the couple was sure that this would be the day that the Chenoo would eat them, but the hours passed without event, and as they told stories by the fire, the Chenoo fell asleep once again.

A few days later, Toma returned from his hunt with a mighty kill: a moose. When the Chenoo saw this, it spoke for the first time—with words that seemed to claw their way up its throat like a death-whisper.

CHENOO: *(hoarsely)* I will eat.

NESOOWA: Y-y-yes, Grandfather. Of course!

NARRATOR: Nesoowa prepared to cut the meat.

CHENOO: Not the meat. Boil the fat.

NARRATOR: So Nesoowa heated the fat of the moose over the fire, and the Chenoo neared the pot hungrily. It drank down the liquefied fat with one, giant slurp. *(slurping)*

TOMA: It would eat that?

NESOOWA: Better that than us. *(to the Chenoo)* Now do you feel better, Grandfather?

NARRATOR: Without another word the Chenoo laid down to sleep.

TOMA: It ate!

NESOOWA: Yes! I think something has changed!

NARRATOR: It was true. The creature was still a Chenoo with an icy heart, but it had yielded somewhat to the power of kindness, which has a magic all its own.

The Chenoo stayed with Toma and Nesoowa all winter. Its voice grew stronger and stronger until one night, by the glow of the lodge fire, it told its story.

CHENOO: My name is Elaak, which means "harmful." I was a man once, but then I committed a deadly deed—I ate the flesh of my fellow humans—and my heart turned to ice. I have not been a Chenoo long, for that reason, I am one of the weakest of my kind. Our strength comes from the number of hearts we have eaten, and I have eaten none.

NESOOWA: That is good, Grandfather. Eating hearts is not respectable.

CHENOO: Hmph! It is for a Chenoo! If I do not eat hearts, *my* heart will be eaten! Soon my enemy, Winsit, will return to destroy me once and for all. But this time I will defeat him! And I will eat *his* heart. Then I will return to my full strength.

NARRATOR: Rather than consoling them, the words of the Chenoo chilled Toma and Nesoowa, and so Toma refused to leave his wife alone with the Chenoo any longer.

NESOOWA: Go. Hunt. He will not harm me.

TOMA: What about that business of eating a heart? I won't leave you. We will just eat from our stores of dried meat and smoked fish.

NARRATOR: But the Chenoo tired of this food.

CHENOO: Has my grandson forgotten how to hunt?

TOMA: Hardly.

CHENOO: This food is pitiful. I will show you how to hunt. Come.

NARRATOR: Toma knew he had no choice. So he and the Chenoo disappeared into the forest. As soon as they had gone, Nesoowa heard the voice of the crow in the trees behind her.

CROW: I've never seen a Chenoo play with his food as long as this one has.

NESOOWA: He is not just a Chenoo. He is part of our family.

CROW: Trust me, lady. That *thing* is not part of your family. I saw it leading your husband off into the woods. I guess you better get used to being a widow.

NESOOWA: You'll see. Grandfather will not eat us.

NARRATOR: At the end of the day, Toma and the Chenoo returned. Toma looked somewhat stunned, and the Chenoo was holding the corpse of a giant lizard, grinning.

NESOOWA: What is that, Toma? I've never seen a lizard so large.

TOMA: *(in a daze)* This was the strangest day of my life. Grandfather made us snowshoes, and he moved across the snow so quickly I could hardly keep up.

CHENOO: It was my Chenoo magic!

TOMA: Then we stopped near a spring, and this giant lizard reared its head up from the ground. I thought it would slay us for sure, but Grandfather cut its head off with a single swipe of his claws.

CHENOO: I conjured it up—from a tiny lizard.

TOMA: I couldn't have carried this creature on my own, but Grandfather carried us both here on his shoulders—as if it was nothing.

CHENOO: True. I am growing stronger, but I won't have my full strength until I eat a heart. Now, cook up this lizard, Granddaughter. We will eat.

NARRATOR: The people of Toma and Nesoowa did not eat reptiles, and the thought of doing so turned their stomachs, but they did not want to offend the Chenoo. So they did as he requested. They found it almost tasty.

Winter passed. The deep snows melted, and shoots of grass began to emerge from the snow. But the Chenoo remained. One day the crow flew into their camp and began cawing rapidly to the Chenoo. *(crow cawing)*

CHENOO: Kaka-kooch has brought me news. He has told me that Winsit, my old enemy, has at last found my hiding place here with you. He is coming to kill me.

TOMA: *(sarcastically)* That bird always did know how to deliver bad news.

CHENOO: I must face Winsit, and one of us must die.

NARRATOR: Nesoowa felt a pain in her heart. She truly did not want the Chenoo to die.

NESOOWA: No, Grandfather! Let Toma fight with you.

CHENOO: Oh no, Granddaughter. The war whoop of a Chenoo is enough to kill a human. It is so sharp and shrill that it will pierce your brain like an arrow. You and my grandson must go to a cave that I will show you and plug up your ears with moss. Otherwise, you will die...and I cannot bear that.

NARRATOR: The Chenoo asked Nesoowa to bring him his bundle, which had hung on a tree untouched all winter. From the satchel he produced two, golden-bright horns.

CHENOO: These are the horns of a great serpent. Take this, Grandson. If you are ever at the point of death from a Chenoo, thrust this into his ear, and it will kill him.

NARRATOR: The Chenoo rose sadly.

CHENOO: Kaka-kooch will show you a cave nearby where you must hide yourselves. I will face Winsit. Perhaps I will eat a heart after all!

NARRATOR: Then a more human look came into Elaak's eyes.

CHENOO: I thank you for making me welcome in your home.

NARRATOR: Elaak began to grow until he was as tall as a tree. Then he turned and disappeared between the firs.

CROW: Okay, humans, don't just stand there with your mouths hanging open! Follow me before you hear the Chenoo's cries and your brains leak out your ears.

NARRATOR: The couple allowed the crow to lead them away from their camp.

NESOOWA: Oh, I hope Elaak survives.

CROW: Either way you're in trouble. If Winsit wins, he'll find you and eat you. If

Elaak wins, he will eat Winsit's heart and absorb all of his evil. Then Elaak will eat you. Either way, you're dinner. Your little "family" act will be over.

NARRATOR: Toma looked down to the horn in his hand.

TOMA: Then that means I must use this horn. If Winsit wins, I will kill him. And if Elaak wins, I must kill him.

NESOOWA: But he is our grandfather.

TOMA: No, he is only a Chenoo.

NESOOWA: He was once a man. He can be one again.

NARRATOR: Nesoowa drew up and stopped her advance. Toma turned to her in surprise.

NESOOWA: Go ahead without me. I am going to pray.

TOMA: There is no time.

NESOOWA: I will not be far behind. Only a quick prayer.

NARRATOR: Toma knew his wife's mind was set, so he continued on, and Nesoowa began her prayer.

NESOOWA: Spirit above, show me a way to save Elaak, my grandfather.

NARRATOR: It was then that a jaybird alighted on the branch of a spruce near her.

JAY: Take the plant you see growing at your feet.

NARRATOR: Nesoowa saw a plant with a bright red flower. It was a type of plant she had never seen before.

JAY: Grind the blossom and mix it with water. You will have to make your Chenoo drink it before he eats the heart of the other Chenoo. If he eats of the heart, his humanity will be lost forever.

NESOOWA: Thank you! Thank you!

NARRATOR: Then the bird flittered away, and Nesoowa hurried to catch up to Toma. He and the crow awaited her at the cave entrance.

CROW: Who was that bird you were talking to? I'd never seen it before in my life!

NESOOWA: I think it was Glooscap, the great protector in the heavens.

CROW: Looked like a blue jay to me!

NARRATOR: In the darkness of the cave, Toma and Nesoowa plugged their ears with moss, and they helped the crow do the same. *(faraway Chenoo cry)* Just then their stuffed ears began to sting.

TOMA: *(cry of pain)* Ah! What is that?

CROW: The war-whoop of the Chenoo is so powerful that it hurts even when it cannot be heard.

NARRATOR: Then they felt that the battle between the Chenoo had begun. The ground began to buck and shiver like it was alive. Their very bones vibrated within them, and they feared the whole earth would be destroyed. *(rumbling sound)*

TOMA: I can't stand it! I must go outside and see what is going on!

NESOOWA: I'm coming, too!

NARRATOR: Toma and Nesoowa exited the cave and stood in awe at what they saw. The two giant Chenoo had leveled the nearby forest. There stood Winsit, the sight of whom was enough to drive anyone mad. His eyes bulged, his fangs dripped with blood, and his demonic horns pierced the sky. With his vicious claws, he had pinned Elaak to the ground.

WINSIT: (*frightening voice*) Now, pathetic weakling, I take your life. I will feast upon your heart.

NARRATOR: Winsit struck at Elaak's head, but the weakened Chenoo managed to dodge. (*crashing sound*) Toma and Nesoowa climbed to the edge of the rocky ledge.

CHENOO: (*hoarsely*) Help me! Help me, my grandchildren!

WINSIT: You fool! Who would help you? You're a demon like me! No one cares if you live or die!

NESOOWA: We care!

WINSIT: (*growling*) What?

NARRATOR: The vile Chenoo turned toward Nesoowa's voice—his eyes blazing with fire—and when he did, Toma saw his chance. He leapt from the rocky ledge, grabbing onto the Chenoo's monstrous earlobe, and drove the horn into the creature's ear canal. (*Shunk!*)

WINSIT: (*screaming*) Argh! Argh!

NARRATOR: The horn, finding its target struck, lengthened until it came out the other side of Winsit's head. (*skewering sound*)

WINSIT: (*dying sounds*)

NARRATOR: Winsit crashed lifeless to the ground, and the impact shook the entire forest. (*massive boom*) Elaak staggered to his feet and rejoiced at the sight of his dead enemy.

CHENOO: (*gravelly and harsh*) I have won! I have won! Now I will feast on his heart! His power will be mine…mine!

NESOOWA: Wait, Grandfather!

NARRATOR: Standing on the ledge, Nesoowa raised a birch-bark cup of water into which she had mixed the special flower.

NESOOWA: Your fight must have made you thirsty. Drink this first.

CHENOO: (*raging*) No! The heart! That is all I need!

NESOOWA: (*sternly*) Grandfather! Listen to my wisdom. Drink first.

NARRATOR: The enraged face of the Chenoo started to soften.

CHENOO: All right. Just for you, Granddaughter.

NARRATOR: Elaak took the drink from her hand and gulped it down. A strange look came into his eyes, and he dropped the cup. His shoulders drooping, he began to shrink back down, down into his former size—finally collapsing into a heap upon the ground.

CHENOO: *(coughing)*

NARRATOR: There Elaak wretched until he coughed up a clump of ice in the shape of a man. The man-shaped ice-clump melted away and so did all the monstrous features of Elaak—until he looked like nothing more than a withered, old man. Toma and Nesoowa climbed down from their rocky perch to be at his side.

NESOOWA: Grandfather! Grandfather!

CHENOO: My children! My children!

NESOOWA: You are human once again! I knew you could return to us!

CHENOO: You saved me. Your kindness saved me.

NARRATOR: From that day forward Elaak lived with Toma and Nesoowa in peace. And when the couple had children, he was the kindest of grandfathers. They were troubled no more by monsters of any size, for everyone had heard of Toma and Nesoowa, the slayers of the Chenoo.

DISCUSSION QUESTIONS

1. What do you find interesting about the Chenoo creature?
2. The Chenoo is similar to the Wendigo, another Native American mythical creature that is the result of cannibalism. Why do you think there are so many monsters related to cannibalism?
3. What lesson does this story teach?
4. Why are Toma and Nesoowa heroes?
5. Is the story right—does kindness have a magic all its own? Explain.

THE HERO TWINS IN THE LAND OF THE DEAD
TEACHER GUIDE

BACKGROUND

Xibalba was the Mayan underworld. Its name literally means "the land of fear," and its nine levels were home to many terrifying sights. Only the bravest of heroes could face it—let alone defeat the Lords of the Dead who dwell there. Fortunately, the Hero Twins are up to the job.

Many ancient cultures viewed twins as possessing special abilities or mystical qualities, and the Maya people were no different. Not only are the Hero Twins the ultimate athletes, but they also possess magical powers. Their story and many others are told in the *Popol Vuh*, a 16th century collection of Mayan mythology.

As for Pok-ta-Pok, the Mayan ceremonial ball game featured in this story, it had a seemingly simple objective: to hit a rubber ball through a stone hoop high on a wall; however, players could only use their hips and the opposing team defended the hoop—making the game quite difficult. The Maya forced war prisoners to compete in the ball game. Then they sacrificed the losers (and sometimes the winners, too.)

SUMMARY

Grandmother and her two grandsons are visited one night by a strange woman from Xibalba, the land of the dead. The woman is delivering her twin sons, Hunahpu and Xbalanque, the children of Grandmother's dead son, for Grandmother to raise. After the woman departs, Grandmother tells her other grandsons to kill the twins. The older grandsons throw the babies into an anthill and into a thorn bush, but the babies are unharmed. Finally, they leave the twins alone in the wilderness to die, but the animals of the forest care for the babies, and they return to Grandmother's hut years later.

The older grandsons continue to bully the twins until while hunting one day the twins transform them into monkeys. Grandmother is angry when she discovers this, but she laughs at the sight of the other grandsons' monkey faces, and they leave forever.

Grandmother gives the twins the job of clearing the forest, which they do by enchanting their tools. However, they find that the forest is replanted every night by the creatures of the forest. Trying to capture the animals, they pull off the tails of the bobcat and the rabbit, but they catch the mouse, who promises to tell them a secret if they will spare him: Their father and his twin brother offended the Lords of the Dead with their loud ball playing and were summoned to Xibalba to compete with them and were subsequently murdered. The mouse also shows them where Grandmother has hidden their ball equipment. Grandmother discovers the twins playing Pok-ta-Pok and warns them this is what led to the death of their father.

The twins continue to play Pok-ta-Pok loudly and soon receive a summons to Xibalba from the Lords of Death. A mosquito arrives to show them how to find their way. When they arrive at the death gods' city, the mosquito shows them the gods have set out decoys of themselves to humiliate the twins. When the twins meet the actual death gods, the mosquito had told them all of their names, and the twins humiliate the gods with this knowledge.

Each day the twins play the death gods in a game of Pok-ta-Pok, and although they could win, the twins decide to lose on purpose to further humiliate the gods. Each night the gods put them in a different deadly temple. The first night is the House of Darkness, but fireflies arrive and keep the twins from succumbing to the darkness. On subsequent nights the twins stay in a house of jaguars, a house of heat, a house of cold, and finally, a house of bats, where a bat snatches off Hunahpu's head. At the match the next day, it looks like Xbalanque will lose with only his brother's headless body to assist him, but a rabbit shows up with a melon to use for Hunahpu's head and helps rescue the actual head. The twins win decisively, shaming the death gods for good. They return to earth victorious.

ESSENTIAL QUESTION

- Should we live in fear of death?

NAME PRONUNCIATIONS

Hunahpu	HOO-NUH-POO
Xbalanque	SHEE-BAH-LUN-KĀ
Xibalba	SHEE-BAHL-BUH
Xquic	SQUIK
Pok-ta-Pok	POK-TUH-POK

CREATURE FEATURE

The Lords of Death The twelve Mayan death gods symbolize different forms of sickness and misfortune, and their grisly names reflect this. Their defeat at the hands of the Hero Twins is symbolically the defeat of death.

ANTICIPATORY QUESTIONS

- What are some different stories about the underworld, the land of the dead?
- What are some details you know about Mayan culture?

TEACHABLE TERMS

- **Folktale Motif: Unusual Birth** On pg. 116 the twins' mother tells how they were conceived when the decapitated head of their father spit upon her.
- **Folktale Motif: Animal Origins** On pg. 118 the older grandsons turn into the first monkeys. On pg. 119 this event explains why the bobcat and rabbit have a stubby tail and why a mouse's tail is hairless.
- **Culture: Human Sacrifice** The Hero Twins challenge the death gods in order to abolish human sacrifice. At one point in time, human sacrifice was a part of Mayan religious ceremonies, and this story probably represents a cultural shift away from this grisly tradition.

RECALL QUESTIONS

1. How do the twins rid themselves of the older grandsons who bully them?
2. What secret has Grandmother been keeping from the twins?
3. What kind of creature helps lead the twins into Xibalba?
4. What are two houses that the Lords of Death use in an attempt to kill the twins?
5. Why does a rabbit bring Xbalanque a melon?

THE HERO TWINS
IN THE LAND OF THE DEAD

CAST

HUNAHPU	*Heroic Twin*
XBALANQUE	*Heroic Twin*
GRANDMOTHER	*The Twins' Guardian*
WOMAN	*Mother of the Twins*
GRANDSON ONE	*Older Bully*
GRANDSON TWO	*Older Bully*
ONE DEATH	*Lord of the Dead*
SEVEN DEATH	*Lord of the Dead*
MOUSE	*Small Rodent*
MOSQUITO	*Pesky Insect*
RABBIT	*Swift Mammal*

NARRATOR: Outside the hut, the wind was wailing as if all the souls of the dead had escaped their graves. *(storm sounds)* Inside the hut, Grandmother poked the fire irritably, while her two young grandsons huddled nearby.

GRANDSON ONE: Grandmother, what is all this noise? Do you think it's…the Lords of Death?

GRANDMOTHER: *(irritated)* It's just a storm! Nothing more.

GRANDSON TWO: But you said sometimes the Lords of Death become angry with us above-ground people.

GRANDMOTHER: Only when we make too much noise! So if you want to stay safe, shut your mouths!

NARRATOR: Just then there was a knock at the hut's door. *(knocking sound)*

GRANDSON TWO: *(cry of fright)* It's them! They're here!

GRANDMOTHER: *(snapping)* Quiet! Both of you!

NARRATOR: Taking up a stick of firewood, Grandmother opened the door. *(thunderous boom)* Lightning revealed a hooded figure standing there—a woman, gray-skinned with exposed teeth and sunken eyes.

GRANDMOTHER: *(gasp)* No!

NARRATOR: Grandmother swung the door shut with all her might, but the woman stopped the door in mid-swing with just the pressure of her finger.

GRANDMOTHER: *(grunting)* Go back below the earth! The dead have no business among the living!

NARRATOR: The stranger spoke with a calm and steady voice.

WOMAN: I do come from the land below, but if you let me in, I will tell you what you have long desired to know—the fate of your son.

NARRATOR: In shock Grandmother released the door, and the strange woman stepped into the hut.

GRANDMOTHER: What do you know about my son?

NARRATOR: The woman did not answer but instead made a little whistle. *(whistling sound)* Two owls swooped through the doorway, and in their talons they each carried a swaddled infant. The owls laid the babies by the fire and perched in the rafters.

WOMAN: My name is Xquic, and, as you have guessed, I come from Xibalba, the land of the dead.

(cries of fright from the grandsons)

NARRATOR: At the mention of the land of the dead, the grandsons shimmied up into the roofbeams of the hut—which only brought them face to face with the glowing eyes of the owls perched there. *(screaming of the boys)* The boys fell out of the rafters and hid in the corner.

GRANDMOTHER: *(sigh)* Continue.

WOMAN: Our world is different than your world. The sun never shines, and the wind never blows. On the edge of my village, there was a strange tree that grew green melons. My father said the tree was forbidden and cursed, but I visited it one day all the same. As I admired the melons, I saw something strange hanging between them. It was the head of a man.

GRANDMOTHER: Hmph. Probably one of *our* people that *your* people had sacrificed!

WOMAN: It was. Its body had been killed, but the head still had life in it. It spoke to me and told me its name. As I reached upward into the tree, it spit on my hand. The head told me that I would bear its children—twin boys.

GRANDMOTHER: I still do not see what this has to do with me.

WOMAN: It was the head of your son. I do not know what led him into the world of the dead, but these are the twin sons I bore him: Hunahpu and Xbalanque. When my people found me with child, the Lords of the Dead sent their death owls to murder me. But instead they took pity on me and helped me journey here. Now I beg you to raise my children as your own.

NARRATOR: Grandmother stared down at the twin babies by the fire.

GRANDMOTHER: I will take them. Not for you, but for my dead son. *You* must leave.

WOMAN: I will, and thank you.

NARRATOR: The woman neared her sons and caressed them gently. Then she gathered her cloak around her and disappeared back into the night—her owls flying out behind her.

GRANDMOTHER: Hmmm. Nothing good will come of this.

NARRATOR: Grandmother turned to her older grandsons.

GRANDMOTHER: As soon as it is dawn, take these demons into the forest and do whatever you have to do to get rid of them.

NARRATOR: When morning broke, the grandsons obeyed Grandmother, carrying the infants into the forest, but soon after, they returned with the babies still in their arms.

GRANDMOTHER: They are still alive?

GRANDSON ONE: We tried to get rid of them, Grandmother! We put them in a hill of fire ants.

GRANDSON TWO: We were sure the ants would sting them to death. But the ants stung and stung, and the babies only giggled.

GRANDMOTHER: I'll sting *you*! Get back into the forest and finish the job!

NARRATOR: Grandmother chased the boys back into the forest, but they later returned—still with the infants in tow.

GRANDSON ONE: Before you whip us, Grandmother—we tried! We really did!

GRANDSON TWO: We threw them into a thorn patch! We were sure the thorns would shred their tender skin, but they just reached up and ripped the thorn bushes out of the ground and used them for rattles.

GRANDMOTHER: They must have the power of the land of death in them! Hmmm. If we can't kill them, we'll just have to leave them to fend for themselves.

NARRATOR: And this is what they did. They left the twin boys alone in the forest. But the Heart of Heaven, the spirit of the skies, smiled upon the boys and sent wild animals to care for them, nourishing them on nuts and berries. Grandmother tried to forget all about the twins, but years later, she heard a knock at her door. She opened it to reveal two grinning boys. One held a blowgun, and the other carried a fistful of dead birds.

XBALANQUE: Grandmother! We're back!

HUNAHPU: See? We can hunt our own food! Can we come back and live with you?

GRANDMOTHER: *(sigh)* Very well.

NARRATOR: But life with Grandmother was not peaceful. The other grandsons were jealous of the twins and were always bullying them and treating them roughly.

GRANDSON ONE: You stupid runts!

GRANDSON TWO: We are better hunters than you will ever be!

HUNAHPU: Maybe we just need you to show us how to do it.

XBALANQUE: Yeah, we could really use your help.

NARRATOR: The other grandsons did not notice as they led the twins into the forest, Xbalanque and Hunahpu gave each other a knowing look.

XBALANQUE: Look! See those birds high in the trees? We can't reach them! Can you show us how to get them?

NARRATOR: Sure enough, high in the trees there were birds sitting strangely still.

GRANDSON ONE: You dumb babies! Those birds aren't too high. All you have to do is climb up and knock them down.

GRANDSON TWO: We'll show you. Stay here, and don't wet your diaper while we're gone.

NARRATOR: The older grandsons shimmied up the tree toward the birds. But when they reached the treetops, they saw that they were not living at all. They were dead birds that had been tied onto the branches.

GRANDSON ONE: Hey! What's going on here?

NARRATOR: The twins were smiling up at them, and they reached out and touched the trunk of the tree. All of a sudden the tree began to grow—carrying the other grandsons higher and higher into the sky. *(growing tree sound)*

GRANDSON ONE: Hey! Stop it!

GRANDSON TWO: What are you doing, you freaks?

NARRATOR: But the twins were not done. As the grandsons rose higher into the air, their features began to change—growing furry and small. *(monkey screeching)* They had been transformed into monkeys—the first two ever created.

HUNAHPU: Hmmm. Nice touch! It really suits them.

XBALANQUE: Thank you!

NARRATOR: When the twins returned without the other grandsons, Grandmother was furious.

GRANDMOTHER: What have you done with my *real* grandsons? I liked *them*!

NARRATOR: The twins did not lie. They told their grandmother how they had used their powers to transform them.

GRANDMOTHER: Bring them back at once! I do not find this funny!

XBALANQUE: Sure thing. *(jungle call)*

NARRATOR: The twins called for the other grandsons, who came swinging through the trees. Grandmother had never seen monkeys before, and when she beheld the strange creatures, she could not help laughing.

GRANDMOTHER: *(bursting out laughing)* Look at those awful faces! Ha!

GRANDSON ONE: *(monkey chatter)* Grandmother, how could you?

NARRATOR: Brokenhearted over her laughter, the monkey grandsons swung away—never to return.

GRANDMOTHER: Look what you made me do! Now I lost the only grandchildren I ever loved. *(pause)* Although they did look hilarious.

NARRATOR: Now with the older grandsons gone for good, Grandmother gave the twins mountains of work—work that she hoped would keep them out of her way.

GRANDMOTHER: Go and clear the forest. Cut down every tree. When you are done with that, maybe I will love you.

NARRATOR: Hunahpu and Xbalanque went to work at once—or at least their tools did. Using their powers, they enchanted their hoes and axes to fly through the air, hacking down trees and tilling the ground. *(chopping sounds)*

XBALANQUE: *(yawn)* This is tough work!

NARRATOR: Soon the entire forest was gone, and a tilled field stood in its place.

HUNAHPU: I can't wait to tell Grandmother!

NARRATOR: But the next morning when Grandmother grudgingly came to view their work, the forest had grown back.

GRANDMOTHER: Ha! I knew it!

XBALANQUE: But—but—it was all cleared!

GRANDMOTHER: Nice try, boys. Back to work tomorrow.

NARRATOR: The twins cleared the entire forest again, but the next morning, it had mysteriously returned.

HUNAHPU: Something fishy is going on here.

NARRATOR: So they cleared the forest once more, but this time the twins set up at night to watch. When darkness had fallen, all the animals crept out and used their own magic to replant the forest. *(sound of animals rebuilding the forest)*

XBALANQUE: *(yelling)* Gotcha!

NARRATOR: The twins sprang out of hiding, and the animals bolted. Hunahpu and Xbalanque grabbed the bobcat and the rabbit by their tails, but the tails came off in their hands, and they escaped tailless. Then Xbalanque caught a mouse as it fled, and his grip sheared all the long hair off its bushy tail, but it could not escape.

MOUSE: Please! Don't kill me! We were just trying to keep you from destroying our home!

HUNAHPU: Hmmm. I never thought of that.

XBALANQUE: But we're still angry!

MOUSE: If you promise to let me go, I'll tell you a secret! I'll tell you the truth about your father!

HUNAHPU: Keep talking…

MOUSE: You see, your father was a twin just like you. He and his brother had a very special skill. They were good at… *(whispering)* playing ball.

XBALANQUE: *(whispering)* What is…ball?

MOUSE: That's the secret! It's a sport that everyone knows about, but you! It's called Pok-ta-Pok. Your father and your uncle played it all the time. But the noise of it offended the Lords of the Dead. They invited your father and uncle to come and play ball against them in the underworld. But they tricked them and murdered them. So your grandmother hid the ball equipment, and she never told you what happened.

HUNAHPU: No wonder she is grouchy all the time!

MOUSE: She also didn't tell you your mother was from the land of the dead. Where do you think you got those amazing powers?

HUNAHPU: Uh…I just thought we were special.

XBALANQUE: Show us where Grandmother has hidden this ball equipment.

HUNAHPU: Yeah, we want to play!

MOUSE: All right! All right! Just let me go.

NARRATOR: The mouse led the twins back to their hut. Fortunately, Grandmother was away drawing water.

MOUSE: I saw her hide it up here. I was a house mouse at the time.

NARRATOR: He climbed into the rafters, where Grandmother had tied up the ball equipment. He nibbled through the ropes that held it, and the equipment came crashing down to the floor. *(crashing sound)* Hunahpu and Xbalanque picked up a rubber ball and began to bounce it back and forth on their hips. They found a wooden hoop and hung it on the wall.

MOUSE: Now hit the ball through the hoop without using your hands or feet.

NARRATOR: The twins did so with ease.

MOUSE: See? You're naturals—just like your father!

NARRATOR: Just then the hut door flew open. Grandmother dropped her container of water.

GRANDMOTHER: No! No! No!

MOUSE: Well, time for me to scurry off!

HUNAHPU: But, Grandmother! This is wonderful!

GRANDMOTHER: Not again! The Lords of Death killed your father! I won't have the same thing happening to you!

XBALANQUE: What do you care? You do not love us…do you?

GRANDMOTHER: Well…at first, no. But after you turned my other grandsons into…*(laughing)* those hilarious animals, you're all I've got. If you play that sport, the Lords of the Dead will be angered. They will challenge you to a death match!

XBALANQUE: Then we will accept their challenge. We will beat them.

HUNAHPU: The Lords of Death have kept earth-dwellers in fear for years. They demand human sacrifices from our people. If we humiliate them, no one would fear them any longer.

GRANDMOTHER: Perhaps. But you can't beat them!

XBALANQUE: Why not? Our mother is from Xibalba.

GRANDMOTHER: Who told you that?

HUNAHPU: A little friend of ours.

GRANDMOTHER: That loudmouthed rodent! *(sigh)* Fine! But when you end up dead, don't come blaming me!

NARRATOR: So Hunahpu and Xbalanque began to play the sport of Pok-ta-Pok, and no one had ever played it like them. The sound of their game shook the very earth. *(sound of epic ball playing)* Below in Xibalba, the death lords heard their thunderous skill.

ONE DEATH: What is that I hear? Is that Pok-ta-Pok? It can't be!

SEVEN DEATH: Those miserable humans are at it again! How many of them do we have to kill before they stay quiet?

ONE DEATH: We will have to teach them a lesson again! Send the owls!

NARRATOR: It was not long before a pair of red-eyed owls arrived at Grandmother's hut bearing a message for the twins.

HUNAHPU: A challenge already!

GRANDMOTHER: Remember what I told you about the Lords of Death and their tricks, boys.

HUNAHPU AND XBALANQUE: We will, Grandmother.

NARRATOR: Grandmother hugged them—quickly—and bade them a gruff goodbye. The owls led the twins deep into the forest, where a smoking crater opened in the ground.

XBALANQUE: Well, down we go.

NARRATOR: As the twins journeyed below the earth, the light of the sun faded, but another sickly, green light filled the air. Although they were underground, there were ghostly trees, barren plains, and dark mountains in the distance.

XBALANQUE: Xibalba is bigger than I thought. How will we find the Lords of Death?

HUNAHPU: Ouch!

NARRATOR: Hunahpu looked down. A mosquito rested upon his arm—casually removing its nose from his skin.

MOSQUITO: *(tiny voice)* Psst. Before you swat me, know this. The Heart of Heaven has sent me to guide you.

HUNAHPU: Then why did you bite me?

MOSQUITO: Hey, a bug's got to eat. Follow me.

NARRATOR: So guided by the mosquito they passed deeper into the earth through all nine levels of Xibalba. They crossed a river of flowing blood, a river of oozing pus, and a river of live scorpions.

HUNAHPU: Lovely place!

NARRATOR: At last they entered the gate of a shadowy city, where a menacing line of forms were seated on many thrones.

XBALANQUE: Look! The Lords of Death!

MOSQUITO: Nope! It's a trick!

NARRATOR: The mosquito went forward and sank its nose into one of the figures.

MOSQUITO: Ouch! See? That's solid stone. They're fakes! Dummies!

HUNAHPU: There's no need for name-calling.

MOSQUITO: The Lords of Death were trying to trick you into addressing these fake statues—to dishonor you. It's their idea of a practical joke.

HUNAHPU: *(sarcastically)* Hilarious.

MOSQUITO: I'll tell you a few more of their secrets before I buzz off for good.

NARRATOR: So the mosquito departed, and the twins passed further into the city. Soon they came into the presence of the real Lords of Death with their gray skin stretched tightly over their skeletal faces. All twelve were seated upon their thrones and chuckling to themselves.

ONE DEATH: *(laughing)* Welcome, foolish mortals. Did you have a nice conversation with our decoys?

SEVEN DEATH: *(laughing)* How humiliating for you!

XBALANQUE: Actually, we didn't fall for your little trick, which is possibly the lamest trick ever.

ONE DEATH: What? That was hilarious!

HUNAHPU: Oh, yes. Comedy gold.

ONE DEATH: How dare you mock us! Tremble in terror as we introduce ourselves. I am One Death, and this is Seven Death.

HUNAHPU: Oh, we know all your names: Scab-Stripper, Blood-Gatherer, Pus Demon, Jaundice Demon, Stabbing Demon, Skull Scepter, Bloody Teeth, Bloody Claws, Packstrap, and Wing.

ONE DEATH: Don't our names just fill you with fear?

XBALANQUE: More like pity. Did your parents hate you or something?

HUNAHPU: We know *all* your names, and we are not intimidated.

NARRATOR: Seven Death whispered into One Death's ear.

SEVEN DEATH: *(whispering)* They didn't fall for our dummies, and they know our names. Maybe they're too smart for us.

ONE DEATH: Shut up, you fool! *(kindly to the twins)* Earth-dwellers, we welcome you to join us. Won't you have a seat?

NARRATOR: He pointed to a pair of stone chairs, but the twins were too crafty. They saw that the seats were heated below by coals, and anyone who sat upon them would be burned.

XBALANQUE: No thanks. We're here to put *you* in the hot seat.

ONE DEATH: *(angrily)* Did he just make a pun—at our expense? That's it!

HUNAHPU: We have come to accept your challenge to a game of Pok-ta-Pok!

XBALANQUE: We've come to beat you at your own game!

ONE DEATH: Argh! Another pun! Intolerable!

NARRATOR: The Xibalbans gnashed their skeletal teeth in anger, but One Death told them to calm themselves.

ONE DEATH: Fine! A ball game it will be—tomorrow. In the meantime, we will be kind enough to offer you lodging for the night.

HUNAHPU: Of course! Lead the way.

NARRATOR: This is how the Lords of Death had defeated the twins' father—by sealing him and his brother up in one of their horrible underground temples. But the twins were ready for any challenge.

The Xibalbans showed them to their lodging for the night: the House of Darkness, a temple filled to the brim with soul-crushing blackness. The death gods expected the temple to destroy the twins' minds, but the next morning, they emerged from the darkness looking perfectly rested.

XBALANQUE: *(stretching)* Ah! What a refreshing night's sleep!

HUNAHPU: I rate that temple five out of five skulls! Highly recommended!

ONE DEATH: How did—?

SEVEN DEATH: Impossible!

NARRATOR: The Xibalbans didn't know it, but the Heart of Heaven had sent fireflies to light up the House of Darkness for the twins.

XBALANQUE: Who's ready for some ball?

ONE DEATH: To the Court…of Death!

HUNAHPU: Everything is death with you guys, isn't it?

NARRATOR: The Xibalbans led the twins to an enormous underground Pok-ta-Pok ball court, where a stone hoop was attached to the walls and hordes of skeletal spectators filled the arena. The Lords of Death took the court against them, and One Death held up a ball made from a human skull.

ONE DEATH: Like our ball?

HUNAHPU: Grisly—but effective.

XBALANQUE: Let me guess. The ball of death?

NARRATOR: So began the ultimate Pok-ta-Pok match. *(ball playing sounds)* The twins played the death gods fiercely, and the Xibalbans were stunned by their skill.

ONE DEATH: *(panting)* How are they doing so well?

SEVEN DEATH: *(panting)* It's no matter! Activate the ball.

NARRATOR: As Hunahpu went to bump the skull-ball, it transformed into a razor-sharp blade. *(Zing!)* The blade ricocheted wildly off the sides of the arena, and the twins dodged to the side. *(ricocheting sounds)* But when the ball finished its deadly sweep and returned to its original form, Xbalanque knocked it through the goal.

ONE DEATH: No!

NARRATOR: But Hunahpu whispered to Xbalanque.

HUNAHPU: Let's not beat them today. We haven't humiliated them enough.

NARRATOR: The twins were poised to win the match, but they held back and let the Xibalbans win by just a hair.

ONE DEATH: Ha! So you have lost! In your face! In punishment, you must spend another night in one of our houses. It will be the end of you!

NARRATOR: This time they put the twins in the House of Daggers, where razor-sharp daggers attacked whoever stayed there. But the twins used their magic to survive. They enchanted the daggers, so they could not stab them. They emerged the next day unharmed.

SEVEN DEATH: How did—?

HUNAHPU: Daggers? Really? How dull. Care for a rematch?

NARRATOR: The next match went much the same. Once again, the twins played the Xibalbans fiercely—pulling back from a victory at the last minute.

XBALANQUE: Whoops! Lost again. Where shall we sleep tonight? I'm sure it will be lovely!

NARRATOR: So began a cycle. Each night the Xibalbans put the twins up in a different horrifying temple: a house of deadly jaguars, a house of freezing cold, a house of flaming heat. But no matter what horrors the death gods subjected them to, the twins found a clever way to survive. And each day, they played Pok-ta-Pok—running the death gods ragged and losing only at the last minute. Eventually, they exhausted all the death gods' tricks and traps, not to mention their stamina. The Xibalbans could barely drag themselves to the court each day.

ONE DEATH: We've got to do something! They're exhausting us!

SEVEN DEATH: Oh, we have one final house that will solve all our problems.

NARRATOR: The next night the Xibalbans led the twins to the final temple: the House of Bats.

XBALANQUE: Oooh. Bats. Scary.

NARRATOR: These were not just any bats. They were carnivorous, man-eating bats, and once the twins were trapped with them in the darkness, they knew they must do something to stay alive. *(screeching of bats)* So they used their magic to shrink down very small, and they hid in a blow gun Hunahpu always carried with him.

HUNAHPU: We outwitted them again!

XBALANQUE: Are they gone yet?

HUNAHPU: I'll check!

NARRATOR: But when Hunahpu stuck his head outside the reed, a bat swooped low and snatched the head right off his shoulders. *(snickersnack)*

XBALANQUE: Nooooo!

NARRATOR: Hunahpu's headless body fell lifelessly to the ground. But then, to Xbalanque's shock, the body rose and began to feel around for its missing head.

XBALANQUE: What? Hunahpu! Can you hear me?

HUNAHPU: *(distantly)* Hey! Up here!

NARRATOR: The bats were carrying Hunahpu's head away out of the temple.

XBALANQUE: Hmmmm. What a strange place.

NARRATOR: The next morning, Xbalanque appeared at the ball court, leading his headless brother by the hand.

ONE DEATH: Oooh, your brother doesn't look so good.

SEVEN DEATH: What's the matter? Lost your head? *(snickering)*

NARRATOR: The death gods chuckled and pointed to Hunahpu's head, which they had hung on the high wall of the arena. The head smiled and tried to shrug.

HUNAHPU: I'm just going to watch from here, I guess. Beat 'em for me, Xbalanque!

SEVEN DEATH: I guess you'll be at a slight disadvantage today!

XBALANQUE: I'll defeat you all by myself if I have to.

NARRATOR: As Xbalanque prepared to take the court alone, a rabbit bounded up to him, carrying a green melon with a crude face carved upon it.

RABBIT: Psst! Here! Take this head and put it on your brother's shoulders. It will do until we can steal the real one back for you. I've got the bobcat and the mouse here with me.

XBALANQUE: Thank you. And sorry again for pulling off your tails.

RABBIT: Ah, no problem. I kind of like the short look!

NARRATOR: After Xbalanque placed the melon on his brother's shoulders, the body twisted it into place. Hunahpu's real head called down from the top of the arena.

HUNAHPU: Not quite as handsome as the real thing, but it will do.

NARRATOR: The game began, and the melon-headed Hunahpu stumbled haphazardly around the court. The crowd roared with laughter. *(laughter)* Meanwhile, the rabbit and his animal comrades were scaling the arena wall to rescue the real head of Hunahpu.

ONE DEATH: *(yelling)* Heads up!

NARRATOR: Suddenly, One Death smacked the ball hard at melon-headed Hunahpu with such force that it smashed the melon, splattering fruit everywhere. *(Splat!)*

ONE DEATH: Whoopsie!

NARRATOR: Just then the animals tossed the real head down from above. It spiraled and landed right where the melon had been. *(reattaching sound)*

HUNAHPU: Ah! I'm back together again! Thank you!

XBALANQUE: All right! Pull yourself together, and let's end this once and for all!

NARRATOR: Flying into action, the hero twins went on to win the most stunning Pok-ta-Pok victory ever. As the ball passed through the hoop for a final time, the ground above and below them began to shake. *(earthquake)* They had decisively defeated the death gods, who collapsed in exhaustion.

HUNAHPU: Now we have beaten you fair and square!

XBALANQUE: You must heed our demands.

ONE DEATH: *(exhausted)* Anything! What does it take to get rid of you two?

HUNAHPU: You must never again demand human sacrifice.

XBALANQUE: And we humans can play ball as loudly as we want to—day or night.

SEVEN DEATH: Yes! Fine! Whatever you want! Just leave us in peace!

NARRATOR: Hunahpu and Xbalanque stepped over the defeated gods and departed Xibalba victorious. The humans of earth would never fear the death gods again. The twins had beaten them at their own game.

DISCUSSION QUESTIONS

1. How are Hunahpu and Xbalanque heroic?
2. In many hero stories, nature itself seems to favor the heroes and help them in their quests. How is this evident in the story of the Hero Twins?
3. In one version of the story, after the Hero Twins defeat the Lords of Death, they ascend into the heavens and become the sun and moon. What does this ending add to the story?
4. The Hero Twins were symbols of hope to the Maya people. They end the ritual of human sacrifice and demonstrate their power over the Lords of Xibalba and, therefore, death itself. The Maya hoped to overcome death and ascend into the heavens to join the twins. What elements of the story symbolize overcoming death?
5. The Maya believed that the Lords of Death caused different types of sickness or symptoms associated with disease—oozing pus, bleeding, swelling, decomposition, starvation, and pain. How are these death gods an example of personification?
6. Pok-ta-Pok, the ceremonial ball game played by the Maya, had a seemingly simple objective: to hit a rubber ball through a stone hoop high on a wall; however, players could only use their hips and the opposing team defended the hoop. Does this sport sound difficult to you? Explain.
7. Xibalba, literally "the land of fear," is the Mayan underworld. It has nine levels and is home to many horrific sights. Journeys into the underworld are a common myth motif. Why do you think so many different cultures have this same type of story?

THE MAGIC LAKE
TEACHER GUIDE

BACKGROUND

Ranging from the southern portion of modern-day Colombia to northern Chile, the Incan Empire spanned much of the western coast of South America. The empire of the Inca has been compared to the Roman Empire for its advanced roads, sophisticated architecture, and imperial power structure. Beginning around 1400 A.D., the Inca consolidated various other people groups into a single society. Exactly how this was accomplished is still a mystery; the Inca had no alphabet and left no historical records. Incan architecture is perplexing as well as the Inca did not have the technology of the wheel. The stone blocks of their structures were cut with such precision that they are still standing centuries later. Additionally, it is estimated that the Inca built 18,000 miles of roads to connect their empire.

But for all its power, the Incan Empire lasted a little over a century. Great quantities of gold made Incan cities dazzling, but when Spanish explorers arrived in the 1500's, they were only too happy to strip the Inca of their power and their gold. All that remains of the empire are its majestic ruins and a few of its oral stories—such as this one that comes from the modern-day country of Ecuador.

SUMMARY

When his only son becomes mysteriously ill, the Emperor of the Incan Empire prays for a miracle. The gods reply by sending him a golden flask and telling him of a magic lake high in the mountains, the water of which will heal his son. The Emperor promises a fortune to the one who brings him water from this lake. Many try, but fail to locate it.

Elswhere in the empire, a young girl named Sisa lives on a poor farm with her father, mother, and two brothers. When Sisa's brothers hear of the quest for the Magic Lake, they beg their father for permission to join the search, which he reluctantly grants. The brothers fail to find the lake and instead they present the Emperor with ordinary water and claim it is from the Magic Lake. Infuriated, he throws them into prison.

When Sisa's family hears of her brothers' fate, she decides to take her llama, Yaku, and find a way to free them. Sisa travels to Cuzco, the capital city founded when the son of the sun god Inti placed a golden rod into the ground. She sneaks into the Emperor's throne room and promises to find the Magic Lake in hopes of freeing her brothers. The Emperor's son gives Sisa the golden flask, and Sisa begins her journey.

As Sisa journeys through the high mountains, Yaku drinks from a mountain stream, giving her the power to speak. Sisa and Yaku encounter a puma, who threatens to kill them, but they are saved by Urchuchillay, the heavenly llama, who tells them only the one who seeks the Magic Lake for the benefit of others will find it.

Sisa's food supply soon runs short, and in kindness she offers her final corn to a pair of toucans roosting nearby. The toucans thank her and inform her in return for her kindness, they can help her reach the Magic Lake. They give her a few of their feathers and tell her to make a fan with them. When she lifts the fan to her face and imagines herself at the Magic Lake, she will find herself there. Sisa does so, and there she faces the three guardians of the lake: a crab, an alligator, and a winged snake. Each of these creatures falls to sleep when Sisa holds up her fan before her face. She collects some of the water of the Magic Lake and returns to the Emperor's palace using the magic fan. The water saves the life of the Emperor's son, and the Emperor frees her brothers. In return for her bravery, the Emperor grants Sisa's family a large farm and a herd of llamas.

ESSENTIAL QUESTION

- Is there always a way to find success in any situation?

NAME PRONUNCIATIONS

Inti	EN-TĒ
Mama Ocllo	MAH-MAH OK-LŌ
Manco Capac	MAN-KŌ KAY-PAK
Sisa	SĒ-SUH
Urcuchillay	ER-KOO-CHIH-LAY
Yaku	YAH-KOO

ANTICIPATORY QUESTIONS

- Do you ever have to bail your siblings out of trouble?
- How do you motivate yourself to see hope in a "hopeless" situation?

CREATURE FEATURE

Urcuchillay Incan herdsmen told tales of Urcuchillay, the multicolored, heavenly llama that protected their herds. Llamas were all-important in Incan culture. They gave milk, wool, and sometimes meat. Llamas were also sacrificial animals, and hundreds of them were sacrificed to the gods during mountaintop ceremonies.

TEACHABLE TERMS

- **Culture: The Inca Beliefs** Sisa's Father states the three tenets of the Incan way of life on pg. 130.
- **Motif: Magical Water** Many myths from around the world feature water that it is magical in some way.
- **Backstory** On pg. 132 Sisa recounts the myth about the founding of Cuzco, the Incan Empire's capital city.
- **Culture: Conical Head Shaping** On pg. 132 Sisa notes the conical shape of the Emperor's head. The Incan nobility elongated their skulls using head-binding techniques when their children were young. Cloth strips were wrapped tightly around the child's head. This produced a conical head, a look which separated the ruling classes from the working classes.

RECALL QUESTIONS

1. Why does the Incan Emperor want water from the Magic Lake?
2. Why are Sisa's brothers thrown into prison?
3. Who or what saves Sisa from a puma?
4. Who or what gives Sisa the feathers for a magic fan?
5. What reward does the Emperor give to Sisa for successfully completing her quest?

THE MAGIC LAKE

CAST

SISA	*Poor Girl*
EMPEROR	*Ruler of the Incas*
SON	*Son of the Emperor*
VOICE	*Mysterious Voice*
FATHER	*Sisa's Father*
BROTHER ONE	*Sisa's Brother*
BROTHER TWO	*Sisa's Brother*
GUARD	*City Guard*
YAKU	*Sisa's Llama*
PUMA	*Enormous Feline*
URCUCHILLAY	*Celestial Llama*
TOUCAN ONE	*Woodland Bird*
TOUCAN TWO	*Woodland Bird*
CRAB	*Supernatural Guardian*
ALLIGATOR	*Supernatural Guardian*
SERPENT	*Supernatural Guardian*

NARRATOR: The great Emperor of the Incas was heartbroken. Although he was the earthly representative of the sun god, Inti, and he ruled a vast empire from his golden city of Cuzco, his only son had fallen ill, and no doctor in the entire land could heal him.

EMPEROR: Even with all my power and wealth, I cannot save my son.

NARRATOR: He knew he needed a miracle. So night after night, he knelt before the fires of the palace altar, praying that the gods might intervene. Then finally, one evening, he heard a soft voice speak out of the fireglow.

VOICE: The gods have heard your prayers. In the highest peaks there is a magic lake where the mountains touch the sky. If your son drinks of its waters, he will be healed.

NARRATOR: At that moment the Emperor saw something glinting in the ashes of the altar fires. It was a golden flask. He reached forward and timidly touched the flask, thinking it would be searing hot, but it was cool to the touch. He clutched it to his chest, choking back tears of gratitude.

EMPEROR: *(tearfully)* Thank you. Thank you.

NARRATOR: The Emperor wasted no time. Roads radiated out from his palace to each corner of his empire, and he sent runners in every direction, all bearing the same message.

EMPEROR: Whoever brings back water from the Magic Lake will be rich beyond measure!

NARRATOR: Everyone who heard this message believed it. They knew gold came from the sun, and the Emperor, as the son of the sun, owned by divine right all the world's gold. Eager to win such a fortune, many brave adventurers went in search of the Magic Lake. They braved the highest mountains—climbing peaks shrouded by cloud. Many of these seekers were lost and never returned. Those who returned did so empty-handed. There seemed to be no way to the Magic Lake. The Emperor lost heart, and people began to doubt that it even existed at all.

Meanwhile, on a meager farm there lived a poor family. An elderly father and mother were the parents of two sons and a daughter named Sisa. Working a tiny piece of farmland and relying upon their single llama for its wool and milk, their father taught them to live humbly and honestly.

FATHER: Remember, my children. Our people live by three laws. Ama Sua. Do not steal. Ama llulla. Do not tell lies. Ama quella. Do not be lazy.

BROTHERS AND SISA: Yes, Father.

NARRATOR: But they had to work from sun-up to sun-down just to survive. The father was old, and the mother was bedridden. As for the two sons, they were lazy fellows, who never wanted to do their fair share of the farm work. They left most of it to Sisa.

BROTHER ONE: Sisa, will you milk Yaku tonight?

SISA: I've already done my work. Why do I have to do yours, too?

BROTHER ONE: We want to go into the village and meet up with our friends.

BROTHER TWO: Plus, Yaku's always spitting at us.

SISA: Maybe if you treated her better. *(sigh)* Fine. Come along, Yaku.

NARRATOR: As the girl led the llama away, Yaku aimed a departing spit in the brothers' direction. *(Ptoo!)*

BROTHER ONE: Yuck! Stupid llama!

FATHER: Boys, look how hard your little sister is working. How will she do it all without your help?

BROTHER TWO: Ah, she'll find a way. She always does.

NARRATOR: Sisa loved her brothers—although they thought only of themselves. And in spite of their laziness, the family always found a way to survive.

The real trouble began when the boys heard of the Emperor's search for the Magic Lake. It was all they could think of. At night, they would speak of it through the darkness, and Sisa would lie awake and listen to their conversation.

BROTHER ONE: Can you imagine if we found the Magic Lake? We'd be rich!

BROTHER TWO: Yeah, we wouldn't have to waste our lives here, working our fingers to the bone.

SISA: *(to herself)* Ha. That's a laugh.

NARRATOR: So they decided they would ask their father for his permission to join the search.

BROTHER ONE: Father! We want to be the ones to find the Magic Lake!

FATHER: What? No one knows if it even exists.

BROTHER TWO: Come on, Father! Give us a chance! It's better to die on a wild goose chase than work ourselves to death on this miserable farm.

FATHER: Who will do the work while you are gone?

BROTHER ONE: Sisa will!

FATHER: She cannot do it all.

BROTHER TWO: She'll find a way.

NARRATOR: Their old father lowered his head.

FATHER: Fine. But, please, hurry home.

NARRATOR: The brothers, full of excitement, packed their things and headed out.

SISA: C'mon, Yaku. Time for milking.

NARRATOR: The brothers were gone for many weeks. When they did not return, their parents feared the worst and spent every day watching the path for any sign of them.

FATHER: I shouldn't have let them go. Do you think they've gotten themselves into trouble?

SISA: Knowing those two, yes.

FATHER: Sisa, look!

NARRATOR: He pointed out the open window to where a constellation was forming.

FATHER: See that group of stars? It is Urcuchillay, the heavenly llama who watches over us. Maybe that is a sign that your brothers are safe.

NARRATOR: But the brothers were anything but safe. In fact, they were about to make the biggest mistake of their lives. Their search for the Magic Lake had yielded no results. They had not even made it past the foothills of the mountains before their supplies ran out. But then they hit upon a new scheme.

BROTHER ONE: We've failed! We'll have to go home and admit defeat.

BROTHER TWO: Maybe not. Why don't we go to the Emperor with plain old water and *tell* him it's from the Magic Lake? He'll give us our reward, and we'll be miles away before he figures it out.

BROTHER ONE: That could actually work!

NARRATOR: So the brothers appeared in Cuzco before the Emperor, declaring that the ordinary water they carried was water from the Magic Lake. The Emperor, bedecked in all his golden splendor, looked at them skeptically.

EMPEROR: I hope you are telling the truth—for your sake.

BROTHER TWO: Heh heh. Of course!

NARRATOR: The Emperor took the water to his sick son and gave him a sip, but the water had no effect.

EMPEROR: Throw these frauds in the dungeon!

BROTHER ONE: Uh…so does this mean that we *don't* get the reward?

BROTHER TWO: Maybe this wasn't such a good idea.

NARRATOR: When word of the brothers' fate reached Sisa's family, they were devastated.

FATHER: Without your brothers, how will we ever survive?

SISA: *(sigh)* I will go and get them.

FATHER: What? A girl so far from home? All alone?

SISA: I won't be alone. I'll take Yaku with me.

FATHER: But…but…

SISA: It will be fine, Father. I will find a way.

NARRATOR: Sisa packed herself a sack of roasted corn and kissed her mother and father goodbye. She climbed onto the back of Yaku and followed the road that led to the heart of the empire.

SISA: Isn't this just like my brothers? They managed to break all three rules of our people at once. Their laziness led them to lie and attempt to steal what is not theirs.

NARRATOR: The stillness of the countryside faded as Sisa climbed toward the teeming city of Cuzco. *(hustle and bustle of a busy city)*

SISA: Have you ever heard the story of Cuzco, Yaku? They say the city was built long ago when the sun god Inti sent his son, Manco Capac, and daughter, Mama Ocllo, down from heaven. He gave them a rod of gold and told them to stick it into the ground wherever they went. Wherever the rod went completely in the ground with no effort, that is where Inti said they should build a great city and begin their empire. At Cuzco, the rod of gold went into the ground and disappeared. So Manco Capac, the first Incan Emperor, began his empire right here! What do you think of that story?

YAKU: *(unimpressed llama bleat)* Blah.

SISA: Well, there's no pleasing some people, I guess.

NARRATOR: They made their way through the crowded city streets of Cuzco. At the apex of the city stood the golden palace of the Emperor. Its huge blocks of stone had been laid so expertly that not even a knife could pass between them. At the palace gates Sisa asked to be shown before the Emperor, but the armed guard looked down at her with a sneer.

GUARD: Ha! No little girl is going to get into the Emperor's palace on my watch.

NARRATOR: Before he could say more, Yaku let loose with a spit. *(Ptoo!)*

GUARD: My eyes! My eyes!

NARRATOR: Sisa and Yaku dashed past him.

SISA: Sorry, sir! I must see the Emperor!

NARRATOR: Sisa found her way into the darkened hearing hall of the palace. The Emperor was sitting on his throne, his head in his hands. He had removed his golden headdress, and Sisa saw his head was conical like all the rulers of the Incas.

EMPEROR: Who's there? Who approaches the son of the sun?

SISA: Sorry to bother you, golden one. It is I—Sisa from the farmlands. I've come to speak to you about the Magic Lake.

EMPEROR: I hope you haven't come to trifle with me, girl. The last two ruffians who did so are now in the dungeons.

SISA: I know. That is why I am here. They are my brothers, and I am begging you to release them.

EMPEROR: Impossible! They must pay for their crimes. They will die, and the world will be better for it.

NARRATOR: Sisa saw there was only one way to change his mind.

SISA: But what if I were to bring you water from the Magic Lake? Then would you release them?

EMPEROR: Ha! You insult me! Do you think I would be foolish enough to fall for that trick yet again? Leave! At once! And take your beast of burden with you!

NARRATOR: Yaku bristled and started to aim a spit in the Emperor's direction, but Sisa clapped her hand over the llama's mouth.

SISA: Yaku! No!

SON: *(weakly)* Father. Father.

NARRATOR: Sisa did not realize it, but the son of the Emperor was lying in the shadows—his face pale and his body weak from sickness.

SON: Let the girl come to me.

EMPEROR: Son—

SON: Please, Father.

NARRATOR: Sisa approached the young son of the Emperor, a boy almost her same age.

SISA: I am sorry that my brothers played such a cruel trick on you. I am trying to make things right and bring you what they promised you.

SON: If you succeed, you will save more than just my life. If I die, the line of Manco Capac will end, and the empire of the Incas will fade away. All our hopes hang on you. *(pause)* Do you think you can succeed where all others have failed?

SISA: I don't know. But my family always says, "Sisa will find a way."

NARRATOR: The boy smiled.

SON: Then I will say the same. Do not let the Inca end with me.

SISA: I won't, your majesty.

NARRATOR: The son pulled out the golden flask, which he always kept on his person.

SON: Use this to collect the water.

EMPEROR: Go, little one! If you do not return with the waters of the Magic Lake, your brothers will die.

NARRATOR: As Sisa rode Yaku out of the city of Cuzco, the setting sun caused the city walls to shine like gold.

SISA: Well, Yaku. We have made a promise, but how will we ever keep it? They say the Magic Lake is where the mountains touch the sky. But how do you find such a place? *(gasp)* What's that?

NARRATOR: On the dark hillside ahead, she saw what seemed to be the shimmering form of a llama—its wool glowing with all different colors of light. Sisa rubbed her eyes. The llama had faded, and where it stood a constellation was glowing in the sky.

SISA: Did you see that, Yaku? Urcuchillay! Maybe he will lead us! Come on!

NARRATOR: Sisa and Yaku headed in the direction of the bright cluster of stars. For days they climbed higher than even the Incan roads ran—following paths that wove around mountains whose domed peaks were lost in the clouds and crossing rope bridges that traversed bottomless ravines. At night Sisa cuddled up in Yaku's warm wool. By day they drank from cool streams that ran down out of the heights. But they never saw any trace of the Magic Lake. Finally, one day Sisa cried out in despair.

SISA: Why did my foolish brothers have to get us into this mess?

YAKU: Tell me about it! What a couple of slobberheads.

NARRATOR: Sisa paused. Who had spoken? She looked around her.

YAKU: I mean, my cousin Chirapa drinks out of mud puddles, and even he is smarter than they are.

NARRATOR: Sisa looked at Yaku in shock. The voice had come from her.

SISA: *(in shock)* Yaku! You can talk!

YAKU: What? I talk all the time. *(gasp)* You mean, you can understand me now?

SISA: It must be this water we drank! Maybe it's flowing down from the Magic Lake. That means we're close!

YAKU: Wonderful! It's about time we get there. My hooves are killing me. But now that you can understand me, I have about a million things I want to say to you! Item one: Warm up those hands before you milk me please. Item two: You could be a bit more regular about changing out my straw. I know I'm an animal, but come on!

NARRATOR: As they continued to follow the mountain paths, the two friends chatted for hours.

YAKU: Wait a minute. So now that you know I can talk, does that mean we're equals? Maybe I could ride you for a while?

SISA: I don't think so.

YAKU: Hmph. Typical human answer.

NARRATOR: Suddenly, Yaku drew up. The path ahead led into a forest of dense trees and vines.

YAKU: Uh-oh. I don't like this. My llama senses are tingling.

SISA: We have to! There's no other way.

NARRATOR: As they passed into the darkness of the forest, Yaku looked around nervously.

SISA: Don't be afraid.

YAKU: That's easy for you to say. You're not bringing up the bottom of the food chain.

SISA: If you're at the bottom, who's at the top?

PUMA: I am.

NARRATOR: An enormous puma was reclining lazily on a branch above them.

YAKU: Yikes! That's one big kitty! See? I told you!

PUMA: Hmmm. It looks like I have *two* delicacies to choose from—a human and a walking sack of llama-chops.

NARRATOR: Sisa faced the puma fearlessly.

SISA: We're not afraid of you.

PUMA: You should be. What are you doing so high up in the mountains?

SISA: We are going to the Magic Lake. Can you help us find it?

YAKU: *(whispering)* Sisa, you don't ask the man-eating cat for directions.

PUMA: I know where the Magic Lake is, but there's no way a couple of creampuffs like you could drink any of its water. It's protected by three guardians—a giant crab, an alligator, and the worst of all, a feathered serpent. All of them could rip you to shreds. That is, if I wasn't going to do that first…

YAKU: I'd like to see you try! Ever heard of B.L.S.? Berserk Llama Syndrome? Just watch yourself, tabby!

PUMA: *(big cat screech)* Raar!

NARRATOR: The puma sprang forward, but Yaku let loose with a spit. *(Ptoo!)* The spit caught the puma in mid-jump.

PUMA: Rargh!

YAKU: *(screaming)* Run!

NARRATOR: With Sisa clinging to her neck, Yaku ran for all she was worth, leaving the forest far behind. Finally, after miles and miles, Yaku fell to the ground in a heap.

YAKU: *(out of breath)* I think we lost him!

NARRATOR: Evening was falling, and a not-so-distant growling filled the night air. *(large cat yell in the distance)*

YAKU: Don't say it.

SISA: That sounds like the puma.

YAKU: I told you not to say it!

NARRATOR: They backed themselves up against the mountainside, and sure enough, the yellow eyes of the puma appeared in the darkness before them.

YAKU: Well, goodbye, Sisa! I'll miss our chats! Especially since they're not so one-sided anymore!

PUMA: It's the end of the road, meat-bags! Spit all you want! Now I have you!

NARRATOR: As the puma prepared to spring, Sisa and Yaku braced themselves for the inevitable. But suddenly a bright light came rocketing down out of the sky. *(Shoom!)* It touched down in a fiery blaze before them and solidified into the form of a heavenly llama, its fur glowing with all the colors of the rainbow. *(heavenly sound)* The llama kicked out its hind legs at the puma—sending it squalling away into the darkness.

PUMA: *(cry of pain)* Reer!

NARRATOR: The llama turned its starry eyes upon Yaku and Sisa, and the little girl bowed her head respectfully.

SISA: Thank you!

YAKU: Oh my! The heavenly llama! What a star—or a group of stars actually. And here I am without my autograph book!

URCUCHILLAY: Greetings, travelers! I have watched over your journey so far. You are nearer your destination than ever before.

SISA: Can you tell us how to find the Magic Lake?

YAKU: Yeah, or maybe just zap us the rest of the way there?

URCUCHILLAY: I cannot. But I can tell you this. Only the one who seeks the lake for the good of others, and not for selfish ambition, can find a way. And your kindness will be the key to your success.

YAKU: So that's a "no" to teleporting us the rest of the way?

NARRATOR: Urcuchillay simply smiled. His fur began to sparkle, and he rose upward and dissolved back into the night sky.

YAKU: Whoa! That guy knows how to make an entrance *and* an exit!

SISA: Did you hear what he said? We must be close!

NARRATOR: As morning broke, they continued their journey. But days passed, and the lake never presented itself. Then one morning Sisa looked into her provisions, and a sad reality broke upon her.

SISA: My corn is almost gone. *(tearing up)* It's over! We can't continue. My brothers will die in prison, and my parents will die of grief. I thought I could find a way, but I failed.

YAKU: *(tearing up)* Don't you cry…or I'll cry!

(squawking of toucans)

NARRATOR: Two toucans were nesting in the nearby bushes.

YAKU: Do you two mind? We're having a moment here!

SISA: I guess I might as well share my last meal.

NARRATOR: Sisa spread the last bit of the corn out on the ground and called to them. The toucans flew down and began to happily eat up the crumbs.

TOUCAN ONE: Thank you, little human child.

TOUCAN TWO: We haven't had corn in quite a while.

TOUCAN ONE: We also like how you handled that pesky cat.

TOUCAN TWO: Of course, it seems a heavenly llama helped with that.

YAKU: Do you two always do that? That rhyming thing?

TOUCAN ONE: What is this rhyming thing of which you speak?

TOUCAN TWO: Words just come out when we open our beak.

YAKU: Okay, Sisa. If I'm this annoying, you have my permission to sew my mouth shut.

SISA: We were searching for the Magic Lake, but we were never able to find it.

TOUCAN ONE: Magic Lake? Magic Lake? We can get you there in two shakes…

TOUCAN TWO: Of a birdie's tail—that's all it takes!

SISA: How do I get there?

TOUCAN ONE: We'll give you our feathers. You'll need some of those.

TOUCAN TWO: Then they'll take you far! Just follow your nose!

TOUCAN ONE: Here! Take some of our feathers. You'll need just a few.

TOUCAN TWO: Be gentle! Ouch! Ouch! I think that will do.

TOUCAN ONE: Now group them together—just like a fan.

TOUCAN TWO: Then imagine you're flying—just like a toucan.

SISA: A fan of feathers! Thank you!

TOUCAN ONE: They're more than just feathers of black, yellow, and orange.

YAKU: Oh finally. They can't rhyme with "orange!"

TOUCAN TWO: They're magic feathers that are…all your'ns…

YAKU: I give up. Okay. Thank you, obnoxious birds. We'll let you get back to your rhyming and breakfast cereals and what-not.

SISA: Thank you, my friends!

NARRATOR: Sisa put the fan before her face and imagined a place where the mountains touch the sky. A sudden wind surrounded her, and she felt herself being lifted into the air. *(mystical transporting sound)*

When she lowered the fan, she was standing on the edge of an enormous lake. It mirrored the sky so perfectly that it was not clear where one ended and the other began. All the landscape around was shrouded by clouds.

SISA: We are here. Now, we must be ready for the guardians of the lake.

YAKU: How will we beat them?

SISA: I forgot to ask!

YAKU: Those dumb birds were too busy rhyming, they forgot to tell us!

NARRATOR: Just then an enormous crab rose from the lake waters and with its hairy legs scuttled up onto the shore. *(scuttling of a crab)*

CRAB: Who dares approach the Magic Lake? Trespassers…must…die!

YAKU: Talk about "crabby."

NARRATOR: The crab started to swing one of its massive pinchers in their direction, but Sisa simply raised the magic fan, and the crab slumped to the ground lifeless. *(collapsing sound)*

YAKU: You killed it! Dibs on its legs! They look tasty.

SISA: No, it's just sleeping!

YAKU: Here comes the second guardian. Try it again!

NARRATOR: A deadly-looking alligator rose from the Magic Lake waters, its snaggle-toothed jaws open wide.

ALLIGATOR: Who dares? There is nothing you can do to defeat me, the mighty—

(collapsing sound)

NARRATOR: Sisa raised her fan again, and the alligator collapsed into a heap on top of the crab. *(snoring from the alligator and crab)*

YAKU: See ya later, alligator! Two for two.

SISA: This is easy! Now for the winged serpent!

NARRATOR: But just then a blast of wind hit them, blowing the feather fan out of Sisa's hands and carrying it high into the air. *(whooshing of the wind)*

SISA: Oh no!

NARRATOR: The light of the sun was blotted out. An enormous, feathered snake came swimming through the cloud ocean above them—its bright, plumed wings propelling it forward.

SERPENT: *(booming)* No one shall touch these waters! Especially not you miserable, legged mammals!

YAKU: Okay, we gotta have that fan! Hop on, girl!

NARRATOR: Sisa jumped onto Yaku's back, and they thundered away after the fan, still carried on the wind. The feathered serpent took quick pursuit, snapping at Yaku's flanks. With a swift motion, Yaku bucked Sisa from her back, throwing the girl high into the air, where she snatched the fan from the breeze.

SISA: I have it!

NARRATOR: Sisa turned to face the feathered serpent.

SERPENT: *(hissing)* Prepare to taste my—

NARRATOR: Sisa held up the fan, and the serpent wilted to the ground.

YAKU: Taste its what? Wrath? Grilled guinea pig recipe? I guess we'll never know. Okay. Now grab that water, and let's get out of here before these sleeping beauties wake up.

NARRATOR: Sisa filled the flask with the water from the Magic Lake.

YAKU: Now back to the Emperor's palace!

SISA: But wait. When we leave this place, you won't be able to talk anymore.

YAKU: Ah, no matter. What does a llama have to say anyway?

SISA: Plenty apparently.

YAKU: Speech—who needs it? Besides, some feelings are bigger than words.

NARRATOR: Sisa threw her arms around Yaku's neck. Then she held up the fan before her eyes and imagined them in the Emperor's throne room. When she lowered the fan, the Emperor and his son were before them.

EMPEROR: You and your beast have returned!

SON: *(weakly)* I knew it!

SISA: Here! Quickly! This is the Magic Lake water.

NARRATOR: The Emperor placed the flask to his son's lips, and immediately life and health flowed back into him. He sat up and smiled.

EMPEROR: You have saved my son! For that you will have all the riches you desire.

SISA: I only desire the things that will bring happiness for my family—and nothing more.

NARRATOR: The Emperor released Sisa's brothers from the dungeons, and Urcuchillay twinkled in the morning sky as they all journeyed home together.

The Emperor gave Sisa and her family a bigger farm with a large herd of llamas, which Yaku ruled with an iron hoof. Because of Sisa's bravery, generation after generation of emperors drank magical water from the golden flask and enjoyed good health. Sisa had found a way.

DISCUSSION QUESTIONS

1. Why is Sisa an unlikely hero?
2. What makes her successful?
3. Was Sisa right to go on a quest to save her brothers?
4. The Incan nobility elongated their skulls using head-binding techniques. Cloth strips were wrapped tightly around their heads when they were very young and their skulls were still moldable. This produced a conical head, which separated the ruling and working classes. What odd things does your culture do in the name of beauty and fashion?
5. The Incan Empire was eventually conquered by gold-hungry European explorers. Although they claimed most of the Incan gold, according to legend, the Emperor hid away the flask of magical water. What do you think would be worth more—gold or healing water?
6. How can you tell that llamas were important in Incan society?
7. The three rules of Incan society are as follows: Do not lie, do not steal, and do not be lazy. Do you think these are good rules to live by? Explain.

MAUI THE MIGHTY
TEACHER GUIDE

BACKGROUND

Polynesia is a place where water, not land, dominates the horizon. With islands as far-flung as Hawaii and as large as New Zealand, Polynesia (meaning "many islands") encompasses more than 1,000 islands spread throughout the Pacific Ocean. All Polynesian cultures most likely originated from a single culture in Southeast Asia that over the centuries spread from island to island. Today Polynesian cultures span the Pacific, a body of water larger than all the earth's continents combined. As the Polynesians braved the waves to settle new islands, they told stories of the culture hero, the demigod Maui—their favorite tale being Maui drawing land up from the bottom of the sea with a fishing hook.

Not surprisingly, Maui is omnipresent in Polynesian mythology. He is the ultimate hero, whose innovations—from slowing the sun, to bringing fire, to attempting to defeat death—change the world forever. Each Polynesian culture tells Maui's deeds a bit differently, and the stories presented here rely most on the version told by the Maori people of New Zealand. But in every culture the gist is the same: If it weren't for Maui, the world would be a much less interesting place.

SUMMARY

When Taranga, an immortal woman, gives birth to Maui, he is so small and weak that she thinks he will die. She wraps him a lock of her hair and lays him in the sea, but the sea saves him and carries him to a smack of jellyfish for rearing. When Maui has grown into a boy, the jellyfish summon a wave, which throws Maui back onto land, where he is reunited with his family.

Maui, a demigod, has amazing powers. When his mother will not tell him where fire comes from, Maui puts out all the fires the world, so Taranga must send Maui to Mahuika, the goddess of fire, to retrieve more. Mahuika gives Maui one of her fiery fingernails, but Maui wants all of the fire for himself, so he douses her fingernail and returns for another. He repeats this process time and time again, angering Mahuika, who attempts to scorch him and sends fire throughout the world. The gods send rain to put out the fire, and Mahuika hides her last bit of fire in a tree. Maui sees this, takes some of the branches from the tree, and uses them to make fire. Ever after, humans make fire using tree branches.

More than anything, Maui wants his older brothers to accept him. Since they are great fishermen, he decides he must have an enchanted fishing hook to prove his skill. Maui travels into the underworld to retrieve a bone from his great-grandmother, the goddess Muri, who like all people of the underworld are half-living and half-dead. Maui uses a bit of food to persuade Muri into giving him her jawbone.

The next time Maui's brothers go fishing, Maui sneaks aboard and appears with his new fishing hook. When his brothers won't give him any bait, he bloodies his nose and uses his own blood to bait the hook. Although his brothers catch a massive fish, Maui hooks something even larger—an entire island.

Next, Maui decides to help mankind by slowing the sun, which runs too quickly across the sky each day. Taranga sends Maui to speak to his grandmother, Hina, who tells him he must have his brothers' help. Together they make ropes to snare the sun. The trapped sun agrees to move more slowly for half of the year, but the other half he can move across the sky as quickly as he wants.

Because Maui is a demigod, he knows he will one day die, but his father tells him that if he crawls through the body of the goddess of death, he can rip out her heart and end death forever. Maui attempts to do this while the goddess is sleeping, but his brothers cannot keep from laughing at the sight of it. The goddess awakes and crushes Maui within her. People all over the world remember Maui for all the ways he has changed the world.

ESSENTIAL QUESTIONS

- Why should we do mighty deeds—for the benefit of others or ourselves?
- How can we use our gifts to make the world a better place?

NAME PRONUNCIATIONS

Hina	HIHN-UH
Hine-nui-te-po	HĪN-NEWEE-TAY-PŌ
Mahuika	MAH-HĒ-KUH
Makea	MAY-KĒ-UH
Maui	MOW-Ē
Muri	MOOR-Ē
Papa	PAH-PAH
Rangi	RAHN-GHĒ
Rarohenga	RAHR-Ō-HEHNG-UH
Tama-nui-te-ra	TAH-MĒ-NEWĒ-TĀ RAH
Taranga	TUH-RANG-UH

ANTICIPATORY QUESTIONS

- What is the difference between helping others and showing off?
- If you could change one thing about the way the world works, what would it be?

CONNECT

Moana (2016) by Walt Disney Pictures features Maui as a main character. Throughout the film, Maui recounts many of his famous exploits from Polynesian mythology. The villain of the film, Te Kā, resembles Mahuika, the fire goddess featured in this script-story.

TEACHABLE TERMS

- **Culture Hero** Maui is an example of a culture hero, a character who changes the world through creation or innovation.
- **Personification** The gods Mahuika (pg. 145), Tama-nui-te-ra (pg. 150), and Hine-nui-te-po (pg. 152) are personifications of fire, the sun, and death respectively.
- **Idiom/Pun** "Hot on his heels" (pg. 146), "blowing smoke" (pg. 148), and "hot-head" (pg. 151) are all examples of idioms and also puns on Mahuika's fiery nature.

RECALL QUESTIONS

1. What does Maui attempt to retrieve from Mahuika, his grandmother?
2. Where does Maui get the ultimate fishhook?
3. What does Maui catch on a fishing trip?
4. Why does Maui want to fix the sun?
5. What is Maui attempting to do when he dies?

MAUI THE MIGHTY

CAST

MAUI	*Mighty Demigod*
TARANGA	*Mother of Maui*
MAKEA	*Father of Maui*
BROTHER ONE	*Maui's Brother*
BROTHER TWO	*Maui's Brother*
BROTHER THREE	*Maui's Brother*
JELLYFISH	*Sea Creature*
MAHUIKA	*Fire Goddess*
MURI	*Rotting Goddess*
TAMANUITERA	*God of the Sun*
HINA	*Maui's Grandmother*

NARRATOR: Before Maui came along, things were different. It wasn't that he brought anything new into the world. His gift was taking what was and making it better. But it was a gift that he had to learn to use properly.

Maui's life, which made such a difference, almost ended as soon as it had begun. Maui was born the son of Taranga, an immortal, and Makea, a mortal warrior. But when Taranga, Maui's mother, gave birth to him, she was shocked at the sight of his frail form.

TARANGA: This child will never survive.

NARRATOR: So she cut off a lock of her hair, tenderly wrapped the tiny child within it, and let him sink down in the ocean. Because of this, Maui is called Maui-Tiki-Tiki or "Maui formed in the topknot." Baby Maui would have sunk right to the ocean floor, but the waves lifted him up, caressed him back to life, and carried him to a passing smack of jellyfish.

JELLYFISH: What is this? It's not a human, but it's not a god either. He's a bit of both. *(to Maui)* Little one, the land-dwellers may have thrown you away, but we sea creatures will care for you.

NARRATOR: Careful not to sting him with their tentacles, the jellyfish lifted Maui up and nestled him down into a cradle among the sea kelp. At the bottom of the sea, they tended Maui as he grew from a baby to a boy. Then when they saw it was time for him to return to the human world, they summoned a mighty wave to carry him home.

Maui's family was all gathered in the House of Assembly, when they heard an thump on the roof. *(thump)*

MAKEA: Did you hear something?

TARANGA: Probably just the wind.

NARRATOR: Taranga looked down, and standing among her three sons was a smaller boy, one who had not been standing there a moment before.

TARANGA: I have only three sons. Are you my son that I laid in the sea?

MAUI: I am. My name is Maui. Can I stay here now?

TARANGA: Of course, you can stay! The sea has sent you back to me.

MAUI: Good! I don't have to eat sea kelp anymore, do I?

NARRATOR: His mother smiled.

TARANGA: I see things are going to be much more interesting with you around, Maui.

NARRATOR: Although Maui missed the sea, he loved living on land. Each night in the House of Assembly Maui's father told tales of the mighty gods, which filled little Maui's mind with wonder.

MAKEA: In the beginning of the world, Rangi, the sky, and Papa, the earth, were locked in an eternal embrace, and nothing could separate them.

MAUI: Ew. This isn't a love story, is it?

MAKEA: Yes, but listen. Rangi and Papa were happy, but everything in between them was crushed by their affection. Trees had to grow sideways and mountains were smashed flat because there was no place for them to go. The other gods couldn't even stand up straight. They knew something must be done. So working together, they used their great strength to push Rangi up, up, up into the sky and gave everything on earth room to live.

MAUI: Pushing and shoving! That's better!

MAKEA: Rangi did not want to leave his lovely Papa behind, but the gods forced him way up high. To this day Rangi still cries tears of sadness, and Papa quakes and buckles to be reunited with her love. It may have made them sad, but it was good for mankind.

MAUI: I want to do deeds like that someday!

TARANGA: Maybe. But you are not a god, Maui. You are a demigod—part god, part man.

MAUI: I want do great deeds—just like the gods who lifted up the sky.

NARRATOR: Maui's brothers laughed at him.

BROTHER ONE: *(laughing)* Can you imagine a runt like Maui lifting anything?

BROTHER TWO: He couldn't reach the doorlatch—let alone the sky!

NARRATOR: Maui swelled up his chest and glared at them angrily.

MAUI: I may be small, but I'm mighty! Just you watch and see. I'll do great deeds someday!

NARRATOR: His father smiled.

MAKEA: You just might.

NARRATOR: In time, Maui did grow bigger, but always stayed more wide than tall. He soon discovered that he had supernatural abilities and could transform himself at will. So when he was playing hide-and-seek, he simply shrank down into the form of a tiny insect. Because of these powers, his brothers never wanted to play with him, so as Maui grew older, he was always pulling pranks and causing mischief—just to get attention.

Maui loved fire—or more accurately, the cooked food fire produced. But in those days, fire was still a mystery, and not all humans possessed it. Those who had it gained it secretly, tended it carefully, and guarded it closely. Maui wanted to know where fire came from, but his mother would not tell him.

TARANGA: Why do you want to know, Maui?

MAUI: No reason.

TARANGA: Is it so that you can play some kind of trick?

MAUI: Me? Never!

NARRATOR: Maui's mother looked at him knowingly.

TARANGA: You're up to something. That's why I won't tell you.

MAUI: I'll just force her to tell me.

NARRATOR: So Maui went around the world and extinguished all the fires of the world. *(sound of fire being extinguished)* When Taranga found out, she was furious.

TARANGA: Maui! This is serious mischief!

MAUI: You can say that again. I have put out all the fires of the world!

TARANGA: How will people cook their food and warm their homes?

MAUI: Hmmm. That is a stumper. If only I knew where fire came from, I could go get it.

TARANGA: *(sigh)* Fine. I should have known you wouldn't stop until you'd gotten your way. You must go to Mahuika, the Goddess of Fire—your grandmother.

MAUI: Grandmother? She's not going to pinch my cheeks, is she?

TARANGA: She might burn them right off your face. And it would serve you right, too! Now hurry—unless you want a cold dinner!

NARRATOR: Maui set out for Mahuika's home, a fiery mountain at the very end of the world. A deep tunnel led Maui into the heart of the mountain, and there he came face to face with his fearsome forbearer. Mahuika's skin was dark stone, her eyes live coals, and her hair waving flames, and when she saw Maui approaching, her anger blazed out.

MAHUIKA: *(old voice)* Keep your distance, or you will taste my flame, human!

MAUI: Actually, I'm a demigod. *And* also your precious grandson.

MAHUIKA: Hmph. Kind of stumpy, aren't you?

MAUI: Watch it, granny. *(catching himself)* I mean…honored goddess, might you share your gift of fire with me?

MAHUIKA: Why should I? It's mine!

MAUI: Well…uh…all the fire we had went out.

MAHUIKA: Wasted it, huh? I should have known! That's typical of a youngster human like you!

MAUI: Demigod.

MAHUIKA: You know, back in my day, a bit of flame went further than it does now. We had to work harder for it, too!

MAUI: *(under his breath)* Old battleaxe. *(out loud)* Soooo...are you going to give me fire or not?

MAHUIKA: Very well—but just a little blaze.

NARRATOR: Mahuika held up her hand. Upon each fingertip burned a fiery fingernail. She pulled one of them loose and handed it to Maui.

MAHUIKA: Now scram! And don't let me see you around here again, whippersnapper.

NARRATOR: Maui marched triumphantly away with the flame in his grip. But then he began to think.

MAUI: Why should that old crank get to keep fire? What if I took all of her fire and gave it to the humans? Then I'll be known far and wide as Maui the firebringer! That has quite a ring to it!

NARRATOR: So he doused the fire fingernail in a stream and went back to Mahuika.

MAUI: Sorry, Grandmother, I...uh...dropped that fingernail in the stream as I crossed. Could I have another?

MAHUIKA: What? Give you more fire?

MAUI: Yes, it's just that I'm so young and irresponsible! I'll do better next time.

NARRATOR: So Mahuika pulled out another one of her fingernails. But as soon as Maui left the cave, he doused it, too, and returned with another excuse.

MAUI: Just call me butterfingers! I dropped it again!

MAHUIKA: All right. One more, I guess.

NARRATOR: Maui repeated this trick until Mahuika had pulled out all but one of her fingernails. When he returned for the tenth time, she flew into a rage.

MAHUIKA: Again? No! No!

MAUI: C'mon, granny. You have to admit you need a bit of a manicure—and possibly a shave.

MAHUIKA: You ungrateful brat! You want fire? I'll give you fire!

NARRATOR: Her mouth opened like a furnace and spewed fire toward him, but the demigod quickly transformed into an eagle. *(sounds of a blaze, eagle screech)* He soared out of her cave with Mahuika hot on his heels.

MAHUIKA: Get back here, you little monster!

NARRATOR: Safely away, Maui watched in shock as the fire spread throughout the forests, and soon the whole earth was burning. By the time Maui made it home, even the sea was boiling.

TARANGA: Maui! What did you do?

MAUI: Let's just say the family reunion did not go so well.

TARANGA: Go and beg your grandmother's forgiveness, young man, while I try to do something about this fire.

NARRATOR: So Taranga called out to Rangi, the god of the sky, and he rained down upon the earth, putting out the raging flames. *(storm sounds)* Soaring on the wings of an eagle, Maui neared Mahuika's mountain, where he saw his grandmother fleeing from the falling rain.

MAHUIKA: Gah! This rain will douse my precious flames!

NARRATOR: So she hid the sparks of her final fingernail in the wood of the nearby trees. Maui spied this from above, and when he returned to the people of his village, he carried two branches from these trees.

MAUI: Tired of getting your fire from the gods? Behold!

NARRATOR: Rubbing the two branches together, he produced sparks. *(murmuring from the people)* From then on, people no longer had to go to the gods for fire. They could make fire from rubbing branches together.

Yet no matter what Maui did, there were three people who were not impressed—his brothers.

MAUI: So what do you think of me now? I got enough fire for everyone!

BROTHER THREE: Big deal!

BROTHER TWO: Yeah, good job… burning down the whole world!

NARRATOR: Maui's brothers were expert fishermen, but they never let him come along on their fishing trips.

MAUI: Maybe if I could prove what a great fisherman I am, they would accept me. What I need is a special hook!

NARRATOR: Everyone knew the best kind of hooks came from the bones of a respectable elder. But Maui would need the absolute best hook to out-fish his brothers— one from a supernatural being.

One night after everyone in Maui's household had gone to bed, he saw his mother walking out of their home carrying a bowl of food.

MAUI: I wonder what she's up to…

NARRATOR: Maui quietly transformed into a pigeon and flew along behind her. He watched in surprise as his mother lifted up a clump of grass from the ground— revealing a portal to the underworld.

MAUI: Ahem! Going somewhere, Mother?

TARANGA: Am I the mother of a talking pigeon now?

MAUI: Oh yeah.

NARRATOR: Maui transformed back into his human self. His mother did not seem too surprised to see him there.

TARANGA: If you must know…

MAUI: I must…

TARANGA: I am taking this food to your great-grandmother Muri in the land of the dead. It is a place of wonder and magic, but the food is not the best. So every night I bring her some of our leftovers.

MAUI: The land of the dead, eh? Interesting. I've always wanted to meet more of my relatives.

TARANGA: Really? Even after the last one you met tried to kill you?

MAUI: Ah. She was just blowing smoke—or actually fire.

TARANGA: Fine, Maui. But *please* do nothing to offend this relative.

NARRATOR: She gave Maui the food, and Maui shimmied down in the portal to Rarohenga, the underworld. In that subterranean land, all the people were half living and half dead—one side of their bodies healthy and the other decayed. Maui explored a bit—taking in all the sights of the strange, subterranean land.

MAUI: No need to hurry, I guess. I want my ancestor to be good and hungry when I arrive with this food, and I'll use that to my advantage!

NARRATOR: Finally, he arrived before the goddess, Muri. Her form was frightening—a bloated giant with frizzled hair—half-rotten and clotted with gore. Her gelatinous stomach spilled onto the ground before her, and it rumbled like thunder at the sight of the food Maui held. *(growling stomach)*

MURI: Foooooood! Get in my belly!

MAUI: Oh my! Sounds like someone is hungry!

MURI: It's about time! I don't know who you are, and I frankly don't care. A few hours ago, I decided I would just gobble up the food *and* the delivery person!

MAUI: Tsk. Tsk. Family shouldn't eat family. I am your relative. Plus, I am speedy, and you look…not so speedy. I guess you could call me fast food.

MURI: Grrrr. Just give me the food. A little hamhock like you wouldn't make much of a side dish anyway.

NARRATOR: As the goddess spoke, Maui eyed the goddess's exposed jawbone, showing through the rotted flesh of her cheek. It would make an excellent fish hook.

MAUI: I'll give you this food…if you give *me* that jawbone of yours—the decomposing one, that is.

MURI: Fine! Take it! I can chew on the other side anyway. Just give me the fooood!

NARRATOR: So the goddess yanked her jawbone out of her cheek, flung it at Maui, and dove onto the food. *(smacking sounds)*

MAUI: Yeesh. Some people have no table manners.

NARRATOR: When Maui returned to the world above, he kept the jawbone a secret from his family—especially his brothers. He found them on the beach, preparing to launch their canoe.

MAUI: Going on a fishing trip?

BROTHER ONE: Yes…without you.

NARRATOR: They sailed away quickly, but Maui transformed into a bug and clung to the side of their boat until they were far out to sea. Then he materialized in front of them.

BROTHER TWO: Maui! We told you to stay home!

BROTHER THREE: Let him stay. We'll outfish him easily.

MAUI: Oh, not this time.

NARRATOR: From beneath his loincloth, Maui produced the jawbone-hook. The brothers stared at it in wonder.

MAUI: Presenting…the ultimate fishing hook! Ignore the gunk on it. Now you will see the ultimate fisherman at work. All I need is a bit of bait.

NARRATOR: The brothers had a gourd full of grisly guts to use as bait, but they refused to give Maui any.

MAUI: Not to worry.

NARRATOR: Maui took his fishhook and smashed it into his nose, which gushed blood. Dousing his hook in the blood, he attached it to a line, and lowered it over the side of the canoe. Maui pinched his nose to staunch the bleeding.

MAUI: *(holding his nose)* Game on, brothers.

NARRATOR: It did not take long for the brothers to haul up a monster of a fish—one so large that it almost capsized their canoe. *(cheering from the brothers)*

MAUI: You call that a catch? Psh-sha. That's a minnow compared to what I'm going to reel in.

NARRATOR: Maui's brothers laughed at his boast, but just then his line went taut, and the force of the catch at the other end almost dragged the canoe down into the water. *(cries of shock from the brothers)*

MAUI: *(grunting)* This… must… be… quite… a… catch!

NARRATOR: The weight of his catch was so much, it pulled the canoe lower and lower in the water. But Maui held on tightly.

BROTHER ONE: Cut it loose, or it will sink us!

NARRATOR: The brothers threw their own fish back into the water and cried out for Maui to stop hauling up his catch. But he wouldn't. The veins bulged out of his forehead, and the sweat ran freely as he hauled up the catch, inch by inch.

Then finally, it broke the surface. *(splashing sound)* The shadow of it filled their vision. It looked like an enormous fish with its mouth wide open. *(brothers cry out in fright)* But it was not a fish at all. It was an entire island. When Maui's brothers beheld it, their mouths fell open.

BROTHER TWO: It's…it's…an island!

BROTHER THREE: Are those…people?

NARRATOR: Thatched houses dotted the island, and people walked about there to and fro. It was a cursed island, submerged by the gods, and Maui had pulled it up to the surface. Even to this day, the island is called Te Ika-a-Maui, Maui's fish.

MAUI: Hmmm. Let's see. You caught a fish, and I caught a whole island. I guess that means I won! Ha-ha!

NARRATOR: Maui's antics continued, but no matter what he did, it did not seem to win him the admiration he so desperately desired. One day he found his mother preparing kapa cloth by drying bark and pounding it out into thin sheets.

MAUI: What does a demigod have to do to get people to praise him? I keep doing these amazing things, but still everyone ignores me.

TARANGA: Maui, no one likes a braggart. If you're going to do something great, do it to help others—not just to show off.

MAUI: Can't I do both?

TARANGA: Oh, Maui. *(sigh)* Well, look at that. Sundown already. My kapa cloth hasn't had time to dry. It never does. If only the sun would stay in the sky a bit longer…

MAUI: That's it! I'll fix the sun!

NARRATOR: Tama-nui-te-ra, the sun, appeared spectacularly every morning in his flowing, red robes—shining his glorious light over the earth. But as soon as he had risen, he would hitch up his robe and run across the sky as swiftly as his sixteen long legs could carry him. Before the people on earth knew it, the sun was across the sky, his light was fading, and they were left in darkness. Life was hard for people with dusk and dawn only a small time apart. There simply wasn't enough time to work or play before light was gone for the day.

MAUI: What if I could fix the sun, so it did not cross the sky so quickly?

TARANGA: That would be wonderful! There is never enough daylight to do what needs to be done. But if you try to do that, Maui, you cannot do it alone.

MAUI: What? Share the glory?

TARANGA: Yes! You must ask your grandmother for help.

MAUI: How many grandmothers do I have anyway?

TARANGA: Her name is Hina, and she lives on the side of the mountain that houses the sun.

MAUI: Well, I'm burning daylight! I'm off!

NARRATOR: Maui found his grandmother, Hina, to be a refreshingly normal, kindly, old woman, and she gave him the instructions he needed. In order to slow the sun, he would need to weave long, strong ropes from coconut fibers. At the end of the ropes he would need some hair from his sister to make nooses that would entangle the sun.

MAUI: Pull my sister's hair? No problem! Then I'll have the ropes I'll need to trap the sun.

HINA: *(old woman voice)* Now you don't think you can capture the sun alone, do you?

MAUI: Certainly! Look at this amazing tattoo I have. It's a symbol from the underworld on my arm, and it gives me extra strength. And when I flex my muscle, it even moves back and forth like this.

HINA: Hmmm. What about those brothers of yours?

MAUI: Yeah…about them. They kind of…despise me.

HINA: Could it be because you are constantly one-upping them?

MAUI: Possibly. But they're also sore losers. *(sigh)* Fine.

NARRATOR: So Maui padded back home and humbly appealed to his brothers.

MAUI: Look. I know we haven't always seen eye-to-eye, but if I pull this off—I mean, if *we* pull this off, it could really help a lot of people.

BROTHER ONE: And this isn't just to make you look good?

MAUI: No!

BROTHER TWO: And you won't rub it in our faces? Or taunt us for not having powers like you?

MAUI: Define "taunt."

BROTHER THREE: Maui…

MAUI: Okay. Okay.

NARRATOR: So Maui's brothers agreed to help him, and using their sister's hair for nooses and coconut fibers for rope, they crafted the sun snares.

With their ropes completed, Maui and his brothers climbed to the top of the mountain. It was actually a hollow volcano, and the sun lived inside. Maui carefully laid out the ropes and the nooses around the volcano's opening. His plan was to catch the individual rays of the sun in the nooses. And that is exactly what happened.

The sun began to rise. *(rising sun sound)* As he rose, his golden rays were caught in the nooses one by one.

MAUI: Now!

NARRATOR: Maui pulled the ropes tight and anchored them to the ground. The sun's progress was halted, and he stared around angrily.

TAMANUITERA: *(screaming)* Gargh! Who dares challenge me?

MAUI: I do. I mean, *we* do. We will only let you go if you listen to our demands.

TAMANUITERA: I am the sun! I take orders from no one!

NARRATOR: The anger of the sun blazed out, and the heat began to burn through the ropes that held him.

MAUI: Keep holding him, brothers! I'll take care of this hothead!

NARRATOR: Maui ran forward and struck at the sun with his fishhook.

TAMANUITERA: Ah! Not in the face! You'll ruin my beautiful features!

NARRATOR: Maui lowered his weapon.

MAUI: I will spare you. But you must travel more slowly across the sky from now on.

TAMANUITERA: *(sadly)* But…but…if I run quickly, I can get back home sooner and sleep much longer. I need my beauty rest, you know.

MAUI: Then let's make a deal. For half of the year, you will agree to travel the skies more slowly. Then for the other half of the year, you can travel as quickly as you wish.

TAMANUITERA: Agreed. Now free me from these ropes!

NARRATOR: So even to this day, for half of the year the sun stays in the sky longer, and for the other half the sun passes over quickly. When there is enough daylight to work and play, the people of earth know they have Maui—and his brothers—to thank for it. You can still see the ropes hanging from the sun that were used to slow its progress.

TARANGA: Thank you, my sons. Now I have plenty of time to dry my kapa. Perhaps, Maui, you are finally learning what it takes to be worthy of praise.

NARRATOR: Maui had finally found success, but there was one thing that still bothered him. He was a demigod, which meant he was part human, and one day he would die. So he went to speak to his father, Makea, as he stood guard on the edge of the underworld.

MAUI: Father, life is not fair. No matter what we accomplish, we must still die.

MAKEA: That is why they say, "Men make heroes, but death carries them away." When our lives are over, the daughters of the night come and strangle life from us.

MAUI: Is there a way to change that?

NARRATOR: Makea looked from side to side and then leaned in with a whisper.

MAKEA: *(whispering)* Don't you dare tell anyone I told you this, but in the underworld, there is a giant, grisly being called Hine-nui-te-po, the Goddess of the Night.

MAUI: I'm not related to her, am I?

MAKEA: No. I don't think so. This goddess causes death. But if someone were to crawl inside of her and rip out her heart, death would be no more.

MAUI: And humans could live forever?

MAKEA: Yes, my son. But it's impossible. And if you tried it, you are sure to die.

MAUI: Is she as strong as the sun? I trapped him and beat him. Is she greater than the sea? Or greater than the land? Yet I have dragged land *from* the sea.

MAKEA: The goddess's body is filled with obsidian teeth that chew up anyone who would dare enter her.

MAUI: I must try. Even if I die…

NARRATOR: So Maui went to his brothers.

MAUI: Brothers, I am going to try to overcome death, and I could use some support. I know that—

BROTHER ONE: We're in.

MAUI: What?

BROTHER TWO: You showed us last time, Maui.

BROTHER THREE: We're with you.

NARRATOR: Then Maui transformed them into birds, so they could fly down into the underworld with him. They traveled into the darkest part of Rarohenga, where they beheld Hine-nui-te-po. The goddess's massive body stretched from the rocky ground to the cavernous ceiling. She was massive. Her head was covered in a great spray of seaweed, her eyes were shut, and her mouth, filled with jagged teeth like a barracuda, hung open. *(monstrous snoring)*

MAUI: We are in luck. She is asleep!

NARRATOR: Her bellybutton gaped open in the midst of her stomach. Inside something was glinting in the dim light. It was the obsidian teeth that filled her body.

MAUI: I am going to climb through her, but you must not make a sound. If she wakes up, she will destroy me.

NARRATOR: His brothers agreed, and Maui prepared for his journey.

MAUI: Wish me luck. If I succeed, I will end death forever. If I fail, remember me.

NARRATOR: So Maui climbed into the bellybutton of the goddess, but the sight of him wriggling into her gut was just too humorous, and the brothers could not help laughing.

BROTHERS 1-3: *(laugh)*

NARRATOR: The pale eyes of the goddess flew open, she sensed Maui within her, and the teeth inside her began to gnash and grind. *(gnashing of teeth)* The goddess ground Maui up, contemptuously spat out the bits of his body, and went back to sleep. The heartbroken brothers took Maui's dismembered body and buried him in a cave called Te-ana-i-hana "the cave dug out." Everyone on earth mourned for the demigod. They all recognized the good he had done for humanity. But Maui entered the gates of death and cannot return. So all humans, too, must someday die. There are many who say with a sigh, "If only Maui had succeeded." Yet he had. He had accomplished his goal. He had changed the world forever.

DISCUSSION QUESTIONS

1. Does Maui mature throughout his adventures? Explain.
2. A culture hero is a character who changes the world through invention or discovery. How does Maui fit this description?
3. What does the mini-story of Rangi and Papa explain about the world?
4. In another version of this story, it is Maui himself who raises the sky. Does this seem like a feat he would accomplish?
5. The Maori people call the north island of New Zealand Te Ika-a-Maui, Maui's fish, and the south island, Te Waka-a-Maui, Maui's boat. The tiny, third island is called Te Punga-a-Maui, Maui's anchor. In the Hawaiian version of the myth, the storytellers say that Maui fished up the great island of Hawaii. Why do you think this story is so prevalent throughout Polynesia?
6. The story of Maui slowing the sun is told all throughout Polynesia as well. In fact, the Maori say that sunbeams are actually Maui's ropes still hanging from the sun. What does the story of Maui and his brothers snaring the sun explain about daylight during different times of the year?
7. Why do you think Maui has such a strong association with the sea?
8. Do you think Maui's death is tragic? Explain.

9. In another story about Maui, he captures many of the winds of the world and bottles them up in a cave so they cannot blow. Then at times Maui releases the winds, creating hurricanes to punish the people of earth. Does this story seem to fit with Maui's character?

10. In another myth, a giant eel threatens Maui's wife, so Maui cuts him up into tiny pieces. These pieces become the eels of the world. Does this story seem to fit with Maui's character?

11. Why do you think stories of Maui have remained so popular throughout Polynesia?

DESIGN-A-QUEST   NAME _____

WELCOME, YOUNG WRITER! HERE YOU CAN CREATE YOUR OWN ORIGINAL HERO QUEST BASED ON THE HERO'S JOURNEY STORYTELLING PATTERN. REMEMBER: THIS IS YOUR STORY, SO IT CAN BE WHATEVER YOU WANT IT TO BE! THE ONLY LIMIT IS YOUR IMAGINATION!

THE HERO Who is the protagonist of your story? What does your hero look like? What are some of your hero's heroic qualities? What is your hero's background story?	
THE QUEST What mighty task must your hero complete? In order for there to be a story there must be a problem for your hero to solve.	
ORDINARY WORLD At the beginning of the story, where does the hero live? Is this an exciting place? Does the hero want to escape this place in order to find adventure?	
CALL TO ADVENTURE What event breaks the hero away from the world he or she is used to? Is the hero reluctant to go at first?	
MENTOR Who is a wise character who offers advice or assistance to the hero on the journey? What assistance does the mentor offer the hero?	
TALISMAN Is the hero given a special item? Does the hero have a special power or ability that others don't have? How does this talisman help the hero on the journey?	

THRESHOLD GUARDIAN Is there a small obstacle that the hero must overcome at the beginning of his or her journey? This might be a lesser villain that the hero must defeat or a fear to overcome.	
ALLIES Who are the characters who accompany the hero on the journey? How do they help the hero?	
THE SHADOW Who is the antagonist, the character, group, or force that the hero is struggling against? How is this character different from the hero?	
TESTS What are some events that happen in the story that teach the hero valuable lessons and make him or her stronger?	
SUPREME ORDEAL What is the ultimate task that the hero must perform to solve his or her problem?	
REWARD What does the hero receive for defeating the Shadow or passing the Supreme Ordeal?	
RESTORING THE WORLD How has the hero's world changed because of the journey? How is it better—or maybe just different?	
WISDOM What lesson(s) has the hero learned about him or herself on this journey? What are the readers of the story supposed to learn from the journey?	

ABOUT THE AUTHOR

Zachary "Zak" Hamby is a teacher of English in rural Missouri, where he has taught mythology for many years. In mythology he has seen the ability of ancient stories to capture the imaginations of young people today. For this reason he has created a variety of teaching materials (including textbooks, posters, and websites) that focus specifically on the teaching of mythology to young people. He is the author of two book series, the *Reaching Olympus* series and the *Mythology for Teens* series. He is also a professional illustrator. His wife (and editor), Rachel, is an English teacher as well. They reside in the beautiful Ozark hills with their two children, Luke and Jane.

For more information and products including textbooks, posters, and electronic content visit his website **www.creativeenglishteacher.com**

Contact him by email at **zachary@creativeenglishteacher.com**